Being the Difference

Susan,
Thanks for making
this Summer such a
great experience for me!

7/2008

DARIUS GRAHAM

BEING THE DIFFERENCE

TRUE STORIES OF ORDINARY PEOPLE DOING EXTRAORDINARY THINGS TO CHANGE THE WORLD

2008

Being the Difference

TABLE OF CONTENTS

For Anne, Bob, Charmaney, Elissa, Emma, Fay, Johana, Jose, Matt, Patricia, Robina, Shelly, Shirlene, Sophia, Sylvia, Teri, And Tom—The Most Courageous Individuals I Have Ever Had The Pleasure To Know

INTRODUCTION

Every year, millions of Americans take the time to give back to their communities. These acts of generosity take many different forms. For some, it involves tutoring a child at a nearby elementary school. For others, it involves donating clothing, furniture, books, or some other item to a local thrift store. For many others, their generosity takes the form of a check, providing the receiving organization with funds to obtain more resources to fulfill its mission. Sometimes, while walking down a crowded street, someone may even feel compelled to hand some change or a few dollars to the homeless person sitting on the sidewalk.

Whether through the above methods or others, community service is a cultural fixture often ingrained in us at childhood. Beginning with the simple loving words of a parent, "Be grateful for what you have" or "Think of others that aren't as fortunate," this ideal of giving back becomes a part of our lives, even if only in its simplest form—bringing a smile to someone's face by saying hello or holding the door open for them as they walk through it.

Despite what our parents may have taught us about community service or how many community service hours we completed with our church or school, there often comes a time when something greater happens. We hear about a societal problem and wonder what we can do to help. *Could I actually do something to alleviate this problem? Is it my responsibility to help?*

Even if I did decide to help, what could I possibly do that would make a difference?

Many people stop at the first question and think that nothing they could ever do would really help. Others know that their check or their time will definitely make a difference. And for an even smaller group, the answer to that first question provides the hope that they can make a greater difference. And with that small hope, these people push forward—often with limited experience and resources (if any at all)—and they do, in fact, change the negative situation that first came to their attention and made them question what they could do.

This book chronicles this third group of people—those individuals who see a problem and believe, sometimes with only the most minimal support for their belief, that they can bring a change to that problem. Faced with seemingly insurmountable odds—all the obstacles that come with creating a non-profit organization or addressing a long-standing social problem in their community—these individuals cling to their hope and the belief that one person can make a difference. They truly show that anything is possible. Unfortunately, these stories too often go untold. I wrote this book to share just a few of these stories with you.

Take for example Jose Morales. Born into poverty in Mexico, Jose worked for years in a manufacturing plant to provide the bare necessities for his family. Eventually, Jose succumbed to alcoholism and lost his job and his family. Meetings with others battling alcoholism in his town in Mexico became a refuge for him, finally giving him a chance to deal with the problem that had so dramatically altered the course of his life. Desiring to change his life for the better, Jose moved to New York City and became known in his community as an example of overcoming alcoholism. But he wanted to do more than just be an example—he wanted to help those suffering from the same problem he had overcome. With hardly any resources at all, Jose began holding meetings in the basement of his building to provide a supportive network for those wishing to loosen the grip of alcoholism. In those small meetings in the basement, Jose used his own experience as an alcoholic to help free many others. Today, Jose is the executive director of a non-profit organization that helps individuals overcome alcoholism. What started as a problem for Jose is now a passion.

Stories such as Jose's are numerous. In another example, Patricia Parks-Taylor overcame a drug addiction to now run Unity House, Inc., an in-patient treatment center for drug-addicted women in rural North Carolina. Another example is Sylvia Godfrey in the Florida Keys, a realtor who utilized her professional experience to secure a home for homeless teens.

When Shelly Cyprus saw the rise of homelessness in the early 1980s in her community (Houston, Texas), she took action by creating SEARCH, the first day shelter for homeless individuals in Houston. Instead of having unlimited resources on hand to aid in the creation of SEARCH, all she had was a passion to serve and some time spread out over a year to volunteer at a similar shelter several hours away. There, she learned how shelters operate and how she could open her own shelter in Houston.

The list of such individuals goes on and on. In the following pages you will read the stories of thirteen courageous people who have similarly used their experiences and passion to change a negative condition in their community. Although the stories that follow provide more detail than the few examples above, they are only a glimpse into the lives of the individuals profiled. These stories illustrate the idea that a person does not need to be wealthy, well-known, or well-connected to make a difference in his or her community. These individuals are a testament to the idea that if people use their passion and whatever limited resources they have, they will not only make a difference, they will *be* the difference and make the world a better place right where they are. The truth is anyone can be the difference; all it takes is using whatever you have, to do whatever you can.

CHARMANEY BAYTON
Los Angeles, California

"The very first thing I tell every child that crosses my path is, 'You can and you will because you can do all things through God.'"

In a small apartment in South Central Los Angeles, Charmaney Bayton starts her day at 5:30 a.m. with prayer and meditation. By 6:00 a.m., she begins a round of loud clapping and recites positive affirmations. As she walks around the apartment that she calls home, her clapping awakens the several children that call her apartment home as well. Standing over each one of them while clapping, she tells them, "You will have a great day today. You will be safe, and you will learn something new at school." When she starts counting down, everyone knows it is time to get ready for school. By 6:30, everyone is eating breakfast, and by 6:50, they head off to school. Although a typical day starts off this way for Charmaney and the children living with her, their lives, and her generosity, are anything but typical.

Often referred to as Sister Teresa, Charmaney is known throughout her neighborhood for her open heart and her open door. Her one-bedroom apartment usually houses as many as nine children and teenagers, many of them just looking for a safe place to stay. Some of them are homeless or have just been given up by their parents, while others seek refuge from the gangs and violence that permeate the community. What binds them all together is that they now have a place to call home and a caring adult to encourage them to get their lives on track.

Although some people have a difficult time understanding why someone would share her small apartment with so many people or use her own money and energy to feed and encourage strangers, for Charmaney it makes perfect sense.

As a child, Charmaney grew up in Los Angeles in what many would call an ideal setting. She had both a mother and father who cared for her and several brothers and sisters. She learned at an early age how fortunate her family was and how important it was to help those in need.

"When I was growing up our house was always open," she remembers. "My mother took in families, children, and all kinds of people that needed help. In our house, there was no such thing as 'mine' because there would be people there that didn't have anything, so we had to share everything.

"We used to go down to skid row when we were kids, and my mom would give us a few apples, oranges, or whatever she could afford at that time. We would hand them out to people and say 'God loves you!' My dad never complained about my mom being so giving—he worked two or three jobs to provide for us so we could help others."

Although Charmaney grew up in a home where generosity had no limit, as she got older and began working and living on her own, she became engrossed in having her own things and not continuing the tradition of giving established by her mother. "I was so into myself, my job, and my money when I was younger," she says. "But then I had a job injury that changed my life."

After Charmaney was injured at her job and was unable to work, she began to reach out to people in need. Beginning modestly, she began working with young people on the weekends. Whether it was helping them find a job, giving them something to eat, or just offering a word of encouragement, Charmaney became known in her neighborhood as the person to go to when in need.

Unsuccessful at overcoming the injury, Charmaney could not return to work. Suffering from physical pain and being without the job and money she had treasured, Charmaney spiraled down into a sadness that she had never experienced before. But she soon found that as much as she was helping people in her neighborhood on the weekends, so were they helping her. "If it wasn't for the kids that I was helping on the weekends," she says, "I may not have ever recovered."

Although Charmaney no longer had a job and spent most of her time dealing with pain, she was about to experience a dramatic change that would lead her to give everything she had so that others might have a better life. For her entire life she had witnessed the generosity of her mother but never saw the possibility of taking on a life of complete generosity herself. Of course, she had done her share of helping people during the free time of her weekends, but she had no idea what her life would soon become.

She remembers very vividly the day in 1996 that her mother died. That day led her to what she now considers her true purpose. "I can still remember when they rolled my mother out of the house," Charmaney recalls. "I was standing on the porch, and this voice spoke to me. It was like I was awakened and everything became clear to me—I knew exactly what I had to do. If it had not been for her death I would have never known my purpose."

The purpose that she realized that day was that she had to do as her mother had done—open her home to those in need. And that is exactly what she did. Charmaney went from living alone in her apartment and helping people on weekends to welcoming into her home anyone who showed up at her door.

Over the years since her mother's death, Charmaney has taken nearly one hundred people into her home. Although most of them are teenagers, she often houses women with children escaping abusive relationships and even kept an entire family in her home during a recent Christmas.

"That Christmas, there were sixteen people in my one-bedroom apartment because a family got evicted and didn't have anywhere else to go," Charmaney says. "I didn't want that family to have to be broken up for the holidays so I let them stay with me."

Many of the teens that show up at her door do so for safety. One such person who came to Charmaney had gotten in trouble with a gang and was told not to return to his home or he would be killed. Today, thanks to Charmaney, he is a straight A student.

Education is very important to Charmaney, and going to school is one of the strict rules that she expects everyone in her home to obey. "My door is open and everyone knows that—and they know I have strict rules. I stress that people staying with me have to get an education. When someone shows up at my door looking for help or a place to stay, I ask them if they are using any drugs or if they have committed any crimes. If they use drugs, they have to stop before they can live with me, and if they have gotten in trouble with the police, they have to turn themselves in. I believe in a fresh start."

A fresh start is just what Charmaney gives them. All of the children who stay with her have come because of her reputation for providing a safe place. That safe place includes more than just a refuge from violence and bad influences in the streets of South Central; it also includes the love and support from an adult who really cares about giving them a bright future.

With Charmaney, even the small things she does can mean a big change in the lives of those she helps. She says, "So many kids, before they stay with me, would go home after school and there would be no one there to feed them or talk to them. So here, when they come home from school, the first thing I do is ask how their day was and what happened at school."

At night Charmaney makes sure everyone goes to bed with a smile on their faces. Each night from 10·00–10·30 p.m. is what she calls their silly time. It is during these thirty minutes that Charmaney and the children staying with her will just tell jokes and laugh. Although they refer to it as silly time, it really is a serious part of what Charmaney sees as her responsibility— giving these children something to smile about.

A single parent herself, Charmaney relies on the many fond memories from her childhood to guide her in caring for as many as nine children at a time. "When I was growing up, my mom and dad would take us to the airport. My mom packed a lunch for us and we would sit and watch the planes take off. As we watched, my dad would tell us the planes were taking us to France, Italy, or Spain, and we would pretend we were going to those far-off places. We were dreaming—it was such a wonderful time. Many kids don't have that anymore."

Charmaney's support for the children she looks after often means getting them clothes, school supplies, and other basic things that most children need. Although she has not been able to work because of her injury, she gives all of what she has to the children that stay with her. When there is something she cannot provide, the non-profit organization Hope's Nest, also in Los Angeles, supports the work she does.

Despite all that she has done and all the people she has helped, Charmaney still believes that there is more she can do. With education as one of the most important things needed in her neighborhood, she has long had a goal of establishing a school for the local youth. With the help of Hope's Nest, she convinced the sheriff of Los Angeles County to join her in accomplishing that goal. In 2005, the Sheriff's Leadership

Academy opened in South Central as an alternative school for many of the youth that otherwise would not complete their education.

Knowing first-hand the hardship of being a single parent and the joy of providing a home for those in need, Charmaney continues to do all she can despite having only modest resources. "I believe where there is a will, there is a way. You just can't give up, you have to keep going."

SHIRLENE COOPER
Co-Director
New York City AIDS Housing Network

"It's hard, but it's not as hard as you think
if you think positive."

No one knows the power of positive thinking better than Shirlene Cooper. It was through years of dealing with several debilitating illnesses and realizing the power her thoughts have that she learned what her true strength is. It came, though, at first, as the worst news a parent could ever hear.

In 1995, as the mother of two children, Shirlene had high hopes for the future. Though her education had only given her a GED, she knew that she wanted much more for her own children. She was ready to do whatever she could to make sure they would have the best life possible. But soon she would have to confront the battle of her life.

Two years earlier, in 1993, Shirlene gave birth to a son. She gave birth to a daughter many years before, and the birth of her son brought with it the hope for many more positive days in her life. She had not always had such good fortune; in fact, she had not always thought she could be a mother who would be able to provide a nurturing environment for her children. Her life at one point had been at the mercy of drugs and alcohol—and living such a lifestyle put her, and her children, in more danger than she ever imagined.

When her son was born, she knew something was wrong with him but she did not want to believe it. The positive thinking that now guides her life had not completely developed yet. So when she learned that her son was so sick that he would not have much time with her—that he would not even live to see his third birthday—Shirlene could have never imagined that even more bad news was on its way.

Not only did she lose her son, but she soon learned that she had lost him due to complications from a very serious illness—AIDS. Her son had died after living two years with AIDS and without anyone ever knowing that he was infected. This set of circumstances led Shirlene to only one logical conclusion—that she had AIDS all along and never knew it. Testing confirmed that this was true. She did have AIDS, and she'd had it for a while.

From that moment forward, Shirlene's life spiraled into new territory. She had been fortunate to never have any serious illnesses or reason to spend much time in the hospital other than during her two childbirths. Now she was about to become very familiar with hospitals and what it is like to wonder if an illness will be the end of you.

Two years after the death of her son to AIDS and learning that she also had the disease, Shirlene's body struggled to fight off several other illnesses that had taken advantage of her debilitated immune system. Now, in addition to fighting AIDS, she also had to deal with the onset of cervical cancer and tuberculosis. With a persistent fever of 103 degrees, she entered the hospital hoping to find a solution that would enable her body to fight these diseases and get back to a life where her daughter, not her sickness, could be her priority.

The fever that sent her to the hospital lasted for almost three weeks. What seemed like the longest three weeks of her life was only the beginning of an eight-month stay at the hospital in what her doctors told her would be her deathbed in only a matter of months. Despite the news that she only had a few months to live, Shirlene knew that she could not give up. To fight the diseases and to give her body a chance to heal, she decided to take some medications to help her body defend itself. But with the seriousness of her condition, a few pills would not do the job. Only a daily regimen of forty-one pills would give her a chance. So she resolved to take each of the forty-one pills every day. But after taking the medicine for a while, nothing happened. She did not get better; in fact, she was getting worse. Her body had become resistant to the drugs.

Knowing the end was near, her doctors just told her to go home. There was nothing more they could do. The medications she had taken did not even have the effect of thwarting the development of her diseases. They told her that if they put all their energy into fighting one of her diseases, the others would continue to spread and gain more control over her body. If they put their best efforts and medications into fighting all of the diseases at the same time, the medicines alone would have a fatal effect.

Shirlene could not believe what she was hearing. "What do you mean, I'm not going to make it?" she said. "You're the experts, help me!" But the doctors did not retreat from their position. She went home, even though she knew that would not be the best thing for her. Since she had come so far, she was not ready to give up just yet. "I knew that if I went home, I would die, so I had to go to another hospital that took me immediately," she recalls.

When Shirlene arrived at the next hospital, the doctors' comments reaffirmed her decision not to just stay at home. She says, "They told me that I shouldn't have been sent home, that they should have at least tried to treat one of the diseases." Then the doctors gave her a choice—to choose one of the diseases that she wanted to be treated. The choice was easy for her. With three large lumps under her neck that had twisted her head upwards, the inability to even lay her arms down, and constant, seething pain, she chose to treat the tuberculosis because of the intense physical and painful effects it was having on her body.

For the next six days she remained in that hospital receiving a constant supply of morphine to ease the intense pain. Over the next year, the large lumps that were keeping her motionless were drained, and she was able to continue receiving treatment as an outpatient in her home. She continued to address her illness through home visits with doctors and the support of family and friends, who provided the love and support that began to heal her from the inside out.

For the next two years, Shirlene remained at home with pain so intense that it began to get the best of her. She took medicine at times to knock herself out so she would not have to feel it. When that did not work, she turned to something more powerful.

"I asked God why he kept waking me up with this pain," she says now. "At one point I really wanted to give up, and I asked God not to wake me up again with this pain because I couldn't take it anymore."

Despite being at the edge of life, a sign of hope eventually came. "The time that I knew I was getting better was when I was able to get up on my own," she says. From there she took her recovery one step at a time. "I got tired of having people cook for me because I liked to cook and go to the store alone." This motivation carried her further. "I would take two steps and be out of breath." Eventually she became able to walk without the help of someone else. "When I got up and was able to cross the street by myself, I said, 'You've got this, Shirlene, you've got this.'" After crossing the street, she knew she had just made a huge step in her recovery. So she canceled her rides to her hospital appointments and instead started taking the train on her own. For three years she visited the hospital every day, and since she could now take herself, she kept pushing forward to stay alive.

Shirlene soon made another huge step in her recovery. Having the same doctor for ten years gave her a special relationship with him, and it was that doctor who introduced her to peer counseling. "He thought I would be a great person to talk with others and share how I got through my own illnesses," she says.

Through the process of her illness and recovery, she learned a great deal about the diseases that she had spent years battling. "Now I feel like I'm a doctor," she laughs. "I should have a medical degree. I participated in medical discussion groups to meet with my doctors and discuss medical issues. I got books, CDs, and went online to get everything I needed to know about the diseases."

As Shirlene continued participating in peer counseling, she was also introduced to an organization that she would come to be intimately involved with—the New York City AIDS Housing Network (NYCAHN). She describes the experience by saying, "I met with Joe Bostick and Jennifer Flynn from NYCAHN, and they were doing political advocacy and organizing. I had no idea what that was because I only had a GED. They told me that people with AIDS have rights and that they should fight back against injustices against them."

Intrigued, Shirlene wanted to get involved but was hesitant because of her inexperience and unfamiliarity with the work being done. But after having pulled herself back from death, she knew that she could do anything now. So she started simply by handing out flyers in the community to promote the organization and the work they were doing.

Reflecting on why she decided to become involved, she says, "I thought we, people with AIDS, shouldn't have to struggle so hard. We already have so many strikes against us being ill and, in some cases, homeless."

That vision for making lives easier on those living with AIDS motivated Shirlene to put everything she had into her work. She became part of a group of ten individuals working on aspects of a needle exchange program for drug users through NYCAHN. Her work did not last very long, though, as the funding for the program soon ran out. When it did, she was the only one of the ten who stayed to devote more time and energy to the organization so she could continue to learn.

Around that same time, NYCAHN had been holding rallies to gain support for its housing initiative. The organization sought to ensure that landlords did not take advantage of, or discriminate against, tenants who had AIDS.

"I had no idea what we were doing, but I was able to get people to come out and support us," she says. "They told me I did a great job, but I didn't even know what I had done. I was just bringing a lot of people to the events because I knew almost everybody who had AIDS since I spent so much time in hospitals."

Her efforts impressed NYCAHN's co-director, Jennifer Flynn, who eventually made Shirlene the lead organizer. Today Shirlene is the co-director of NYCAHN along with Jennifer. "It was a five-year process of hanging on and believing in what we do to help HIV-positive and homeless people. It worked for me, and I thought it could work for others too."

Shirlene's work was so impressive that she could have become the co-director sooner, but she felt unprepared. "I didn't feel that I had good computer skills, and I only had a GED. Now I use my GED like a master's degree," she laughs.

One of Shirlene's goals now is to help combat the stigma associated with AIDS. She is doing that by sharing her story and being an example to others. For those friends who once had a problem accepting her, she simply says, "Time is the healer of all defects." And over time her compassionate and genuine nature wins them over.

Today, Shirlene continues to put the full force of her positive thinking into NYCAHN. Her work has gotten the attention of some of New York City's political leaders, earned her a spot on the mayor's AIDS advisory board, and has gotten her featured in *Poz Magazine*, a publication that focuses on issues related to AIDS and HIV. And she is not done yet. Although she still has to deal with her illnesses, her positive thinking leads her to say, "I'm ready, willing, and able to fight them with everything I've got. I think I'm doing the best I can today, and I wouldn't change it for the world."

MATT D'ARRIGO
Founder and Executive Director
A Reason To Survive, Inc. (ARTS)

"Despite what I was going through, I could always escape through my art. I wanted to give that same opportunity to others."

As a college student in the early 1990s, Matt D'Arrigo was doing what he enjoyed most—studying art. For him, it was a unique form of expression about which he wanted to learn more. Soon, Matt would learn that the passion he had for art was not just for expressing himself—it would also become a bridge enabling him to reach the lives of children in need.

The life that he had known changed when his mother and sister were diagnosed with cancer within a month of each other. He decided to put college on hold to go back home and help care for them. Over the next year, Matt spent his days caring for his mother and sister. Seeing his loved ones weakened by cancer took a toll on him, but he was eventually able to find a way to escape the emotional pain that he was feeling.

As the emotions became almost too much for him to bear, he retreated to a place that would put him at ease and where he could best express his intense emotions. Standing in front of a painting easel that he kept in his bedroom, Matt found that there was even more to artful expression than he had experienced as an art student. Every day he would take time away from helping his ailing mother and sister to go up to his room to focus on art.

"I would go up there every day to paint and listen to music—to escape," he recalls. An activity that he had done many times before now had a new meaning and place in his life. "It was very therapeutic for me. One day it just hit me how powerful it was that even though my mother was downstairs dying, I could go up to my room and escape through my art."

Matt knew he was onto something. He knew that if the simple act of painting and listening to music could have such a profound effect in releasing his mind from the negative circumstances in his life, then it could possibly have the same effect on others. His thoughts went from finding a way for him to escape adversity through artistic expression, to finding a way to help others do the same.

The room where Matt had retreated as an escape also became the birthplace of an idea that would lead him to his true calling. "I sat down at my desk to figure out what I could do to help others feel what I had felt when I was painting," he says. "I thought that whatever I was going to do should be for children, since they are natural artists and because much of the funding for arts programs in schools was being cut."

While still in his room, Matt searched for a way to share his passion and newfound release with children facing adverse circumstances. "I thought about what the arts had done for me, and I began writing my thoughts. One of the sentences I wrote down was that arts gave me a reason to survive. Then I noticed that the acronym for 'a reason to survive' was ARTS. I took it as a sign and went with it as a name for the work that I would do."

During this time, Matt kept very close to his heart the idea he had about starting an organization to share his love of arts with others. After the year off from college and eventually losing his mother to cancer, Matt gained a new calling and went back to college to finish his degree.

Next for Matt was a move to Oregon with a few friends, where he continued to explore his love of art while working as a painter. On a trip to San Diego, he fell in love with the area and began to make plans to move there. "I knew I was ready to take the next step in life." Within a week, he told his employer that he would be leaving, and he went to a library to get maps so he could plan his trip.

This journey was not going to be just another trip for Matt; he knew that by moving to San Diego he was taking a major step in his life. To take that major step, he decided that instead of traveling by car or airplane, he would walk. So he began to put all of his belongings in storage. The day before he was to leave, he went to put a final item in the storage facility and found that everything except a few sentimental items had been stolen. This was another sign for Matt that the time for his journey had come.

With only a few items that could fit in his backpack and a few hundred dollars, Matt set out the next day to walk from Oregon to San Diego, a trip that would take him three months to complete. "My experience was a microcosm of life itself. If I decided to stay in one place an extra day or take a different route, I would meet different people or have different experiences that would alter the outcome."

By the time he reached San Diego, Matt was sure that this would be his new home and the place where his idea of sharing his passion for arts with others would become a reality. It did not happen right away, though, because the fact of being in a new place without many resources put his goal on hold.

"I thought I was ready to start it, but during my trip I realized that there were more things I needed to do," he says. "I didn't have any contacts there or business or management experience, so I thought it would be good to get some experience by working at a non-profit or some kind of arts program."

To gain the experience he needed, Matt got a job as a scenic artist for a production company doing work for the Super Bowl that year in San Diego. What started as a part-time job soon became full-time, and within a year he was leading the department. In addition to giving him the management experience and business acumen that he would need to create his own arts organization, his job provided him with many contacts in the area.

After working in San Diego for three years, Matt knew that it was time to start the work of his dreams. Even after the time in San Diego, Matt still did not have many of the resources that were generally needed to start a non-profit organization, but he used what he had. "My sister bought me a book for my birthday that was about how to start a non-profit. I opened to the first chapter and went from there. I filed all the paperwork to start the organization myself because I didn't have money to pay anyone to do it."

After years of keeping his idea of starting an arts organization to himself, Matt was stepping closer to seeing his dream become a reality. But there were still more obstacles to overcome. "My original concept was to create an arts center, but I realized quickly that it wasn't really possible because it would take a lot of money."

Matt soon found a solution. "I set up an office in my garage, and I contacted the local Ronald McDonald House and asked if they would like me to come in on weekends to do free arts programs for the kids." His proposal, and their enthusiasm to accept it, created the beginnings of A Reason to Survive, Inc. (ARTS).

Starting with a few friends volunteering with Matt on weekends, the program soon became much more. Word spread about the work Matt was doing, and a nearby children's hospital wanted Matt and his volunteers to do programs for their children as well. As the opportunities grew, so did the number of volunteers and the responsibilities that Matt had to handle. Since all of the work he was doing was for free, he had to balance fundraising with providing these free programs.

"The first year was tough because many people wouldn't give money to us until we had established a good record of the work we were doing." Matt eventually got the break he needed from the place where the program began. It turned out that the Ronald McDonald House liked his program so much and saw how positive the effects were on the children that they gave him a grant and later included his program in their operational budget. Although none of the other organizations were able to lend him the same level of support, this generosity helped validate what he was doing and the decision he had made to start ARTS.

Aside from the obstacles that any non-profit organization faces in its first year, ARTS also had to overcome the effects of decreased financial support as a result of the September 11, 2001 terrorist attacks. However, the tragedy of the event gave Matt even more motivation to show people the healing and therapeutic power of the arts. To do this, Matt launched a program through ARTS called The Children's Quilt. This program provided small squares of fabric to approximately 6,000 children and asked them to draw concepts of love, peace, and hope. These 6,000 squares of fabric were then sewn together to create sixty large quilts that were put on display near the site of the World Trade Center on the one-year anniversary of the attacks.

Over the next year, Matt faced obstacles that mostly included a lack of financial resources to allow him to continue the work he was doing. "By the end of the second year, I called my dad and told him that I didn't know if I could do this anymore because I was in debt and wasn't making any money," he admits. "I was close to giving up, but he reassured me that

I had a solid plan and just needed to give it more time to develop."

The advice from his father proved to be right. In the next year, ARTS received a $50,000 grant from the California Endowment, which was more money than it had received in its previous years combined. This expression of confidence in ARTS by the donor caught the attention of other prospective donors who now recognize the potential of the organization.

"The grant set a lot of things in motion," Matt says. "Plus we had two years of programs behind us with results to show. We then started getting a lot of media attention, and it grew from there."

Over the next few years, ARTS grew from being just Matt and a few volunteers to a full-time staff of five employees and over seventy volunteers. The program began to include more sites such as hospitals, homeless shelters, and military bases where ARTS volunteers conducted free arts programs for children. With this success, Matt took the next step in his goal of having an art center for children to learn about different kinds of artistic expression and use equipment that was not available at the other sites.

Around this same time, San Diego began a redevelopment project that included an area for arts and non-profit organizations. ARTS received about 7,000 square feet of space at a low cost, which is now the arts center of Matt's dreams. Today, the Pat D'Arrigo ARTS Center—named for Matt's mother—contains different areas where children can explore various forms of artistic expression and also includes a gallery that showcases the children's work.

Of the children that the center serves, approximately eighty percent come from low-income families who have very limited access and exposure to the arts. "When we work with children, the goal is to get the children's minds off of their circumstances and let them be kids again. You can see the calming effect on a child." Matt also makes it a priority to give the children a say in the type of artwork they create. "Each child has a magic medium—we give them exposure to see what clicks with them, and we give them some control over what they do even if it means ditching a lesson plan."

It is clear to anyone who works with Matt the passion that he has for his work and the hope that he has for the children ARTS serves. "Maybe they won't grow up to be the next great artist, but after working on art projects, they will know how to work as a team and to have confidence and self-esteem. Even if we just change one child's life, we're changing the world."

FAY DEAVIGNON
Founder and Executive Director
Angels of Hope, Inc.

*"The thing that keeps me going is that there
is always hope on their faces."*

In a village in the African nation of Uganda, there is a small building that serves a vital function in the surrounding community. Just a few years ago this very building was abandoned, standing as a reminder of the poor economic state of the area and an example of an uncertain future for many of the villagers. The villagers that walked by this abandoned building every day had no idea what it would become. It had surely seen better days and was a likely prospect to remain a relic of a more prosperous time. However, they would soon see this building transformed by two women and an unlikely friendship that was forming thousands of miles away.

In Massachusetts—where this transformation began—Fay DeAvignon herself was in need of a helping hand. With a full-time job and a young daughter, Fay had her hands full. Adding to this was the gradual decline of her mother's health due to Alzheimer's disease. She needed more care throughout the day than Fay was able to give. Searching for someone who could take care of her mother, Fay found the ideal person. Her name was Regina, and she was eager to help.

Over the following months, Regina's role became less of a hired caregiver and more of a new family member. She spent so much time with the family that she, in turn, became a part of it. This bond grew even stronger as time went on. Fay's mother eventually passed away. But when Regina's work as a caregiver was over, the relationship she formed with the family was not.

"Regina had met a number of my family members, friends, and neighbors, so she was like another part of our family, and the friendship never went away," Fay says. After becoming so closely intertwined with Fay's family, Regina wanted Fay to travel with her to get to know some of her own family. Regina invited Fay to join her to visit her family in Uganda. The decision took only a matter of moments for Fay—there was no way she could turn down this opportunity to visit Uganda, the home of the newest addition to her family and an area of the world that she had longed to visit.

Not only would this trip give Fay an opportunity to learn more about Regina, but it would also give her a first-hand look at a place and culture she had only been able to view through her friend's tales. "I had spent a great deal of time talking to her while she was caring for my mom," Fay recalls. "I had many conversations with her about her country." From what she had learned, Fay became determined to make her trip count—not to just go as a tourist or visitor, but to travel with a purpose.

"I asked Regina what I could do because I wanted to do something meaningful," Fay says. "She said whatever I could do for the orphans would be a major gift. I told myself this would be my one chance to do something, and that I could only do it this one time." With that sense of purpose, Fay began collecting items to give to the orphaned children she expected to meet there. For the next few months, she collected items that the children could use, such as clothes and vitamins.

As the trip drew near, Fay realized that there was even more she could do. "Since part of my background included being an emergency medical technician," she says, "it became clear to me that I had enough knowledge to provide some basic health care needs. I talked to several doctors, telling them about the trip I was planning and how I wanted to take some things to help the children there."

In those few months prior to the trip, Fay collected over five hundred pounds of supplies to give to the children. Coincidentally, just before she left, she and Regina were introduced to a group of college students who were also heading to Uganda and who would later prove to be an invaluable resource for Fay.

After all of her planning, fundraising, and collecting were done, the time to leave for Uganda had arrived. Fay's mission was clear. She had traveled a considerable distance from her home in Massachusetts, where she first asked how she could help. Now, with the vast amount of supplies and medicines that she collected, she resolved to create a free community health clinic. So when she arrived, she went right to work, looking for a location to house the medicine and medical supplies that she had procured.

Asking around the village to see if anyone knew of a potential location, Fay and Regina were led to a mother in the village who informed them that she had a place in the center of town that she would loan to them. They went to this building, which was a dilapidated storefront. Over the next month, they transformed that building into a two-room clinic with electricity.

"I had about $600," Fay says, "and I decided to renovate the space. I spent the majority of the month working with Regina's family to find people to help us with the renovation. It soon became a family operation—we all worked on it, her family and my daughter, who had traveled with us."

From there, everything else seemed to fall into place. Within that same month, Fay found a place to buy local medicines and hired a full-time nurse and part-time doctor for the clinic. One obstacle that could have been fatal for the clinic was gaining the approval of the Ugandan government. "That was the hardest thing, but it all worked out," Fay says.

Once all of the renovations were completed and everything was in place, the clinic opened its doors, and Fay's goal was a reality. While she and the others had been working on renovating the building, Fay had come to learn about the Ugandan culture and her role in it, but she still felt some unease. Although Fay had nothing but the best of intentions in the work she was doing, for many of the villagers this was not the first time an American had come into their community. Even with Regina and her family involved, many of the villagers remained skeptical and wondered if the clinic, and Fay, were totally committed to them—or if they were just there for the moment.

"We expected that since we knew people in the community and had them helping that we would have instant community support and people coming to get our services," Fay says. "But it wasn't that easy. I could understand the questioning and mistrust that comes with having a group of Americans come into your community. But we're a free clinic, and people eventually started coming and realized that there were no strings attached."

Interest in the new clinic grew so much that what was originally planned to be a clinic for orphans grew into a provider of health care for a large portion of the community. With this success, Fay knew that she had to keep a stream of funding and supplies coming into the organization while she was back in the United States. Luckily, one of the college students whom she had met in Boston prior to her trip was planning to stay in the country for an extended time. This meant that Fay could leave Uganda knowing that she would have someone there to manage the clinic and ensure that it would not fade away back into the dilapidated storefront from which it was born.

When Fay arrived back in the United States after spending a month in Uganda, her life became a whirlwind. "Many organizations come to these countries and don't stay long, so I knew that when I came back home that I had to get on top of fundraising to keep the clinic going," she says. In addition to raising money for the clinic, Fay decided to take what she was doing to the next level. What was originally planned as a one-time trip to meet Regina's family and to open a small clinic evolved into the organization Angels of Hope, Inc. The goal of this organization would be to create even more clinics in Uganda and provide a mechanism for preserving the culture and empowering Ugandan women.

Nine months later, after founding Angels of Hope and raising enough money to open another new clinic, Fay traveled back to Uganda to do it all again. This time, though, she decided to bring a piece of Uganda back with her to share with her friends in the United States.

"We found all of these older women that made beautiful baskets and crafts," Fay says. "I knew there would be many people where I'm from that would love to have them, so I asked the women to make a bunch of them. I took them home with me, sold them, and gave the money back to the women to help them. Now we set aside money for the older women to teach the young girls how to make the crafts, which helps the young girls carry on the culture and gives them an economic base."

By providing in-home health care, Fay has made another step forward. "We were able to obtain a van which helped us a lot because our nurses were able to go into the remote villages and do home health care. There are many people who can't leave their home. Health care in some parts Uganda is something that you don't often see, but to have home health care is really amazing."

It's been almost six years since Fay and Regina transformed that abandoned storefront into a thriving health clinic. Since then, Fay has continued to open new clinics and has opened a total of four. In describing the significance of Angels of Hope and her work, she says, "We're not just trying to provide health care. If you have a healthy child or adult, they can farm or create an economic base for their family and country. If they have that, they are more likely to go to school."

Despite the odds that would be against anyone traveling to a remote area to bring health care to a rural village, Fay uses the hope that she sees on the faces of the Ugandans to give her the inspiration to push through the obstacles.

One example of this hope came when Fay was trying to open a new clinic. Having been unable to secure a location, Fay took what she could and made the best of it. "We were in what looked like a chicken coop for about a year and then the rain washed it away," Fay recalls. "It was bad that we only had the chicken coop as our clinic and even worse when it was washed away. But the next day people lined up under the tree, and we just kept taking care of them."

Fay finds similar inspiration in the similarities that she has come to see in Ugandan and American cultures. Describing some of the children her clinics have served, she says, "Kids are kids the world around. No matter what, if you give them a soccer ball, a deck of cards, or anything, and if you close your eyes, you would never know where you were from the sound of it. It's just incredible to hear them laughing. When I go into the villages and they come running up to me, I know that what I'm getting is far more than anything I possibly can give them."

Looking back where she has come from since she hired Regina to care for her mother, Fay says, "This whole thing started as a gift to a woman who has been an amazing human being and a wonderful friend. Now it has changed my life." And it has definitely changed the lives of the hundreds of Ugandans that visit her health clinics every month.

BOB LOBUE
Writer, Producer, and Director of
"Visions—A Play About Addiction and Recovery"
Visions Recovery, Inc.

"I used to ask why it was taking so long for this idea to catch on. Now I don't ask that anymore—the journey has been an absolute joy."

In 1991, Bob was a director. Unlike what he would become, his work consisted mostly of directing automobile parts down a chute. As an assembly line worker at an automobile manufacturing plant, Bob had already come a long way. It had been two years since his recovery from alcohol and drugs, and he was now in a place in his life where he was ready to move on from his past. What he would do next, though, would actually take him back through his days of recovery in an attempt to shed light on the possibility of overcoming addictions and to provide a window into the lives of those affected by alcohol and drug abuse.

Bob spent long days on the assembly line in the plant where he worked. In between the parts coming down the chute toward him, he had a few moments to spare. It was in those small moments that Bob had time to think—think about his life and all that he had been through. His reflections often carried him to the darker times in his life when he was at the mercy of the alcohol and drugs that pervaded his existence. But now, during those small moments on the assembly line, Bob was living proof that one can become better.

These reflections led Bob to a realization—that many people had no idea what it was like for him to overcome his addictions. His family and close friends had been there and experienced some of the dark times and often suffered through them with him. But what about those individuals who were still addicted and struggling to overcome? What about the families that were also dealing with loved ones' addictions? How could they be shown that recovery is always possible? Bob's revelations led him to one conclusion—that he would write what his struggle through recovery was like from his point of view and his family's.

So in those small moments, the time between the pieces coming down the assembly line that Bob was responsible for moving, he began to write. He wrote one sentence, and a part on the assembly line would reach him. Then a few more sentences, and another part on the assembly line arrived. He kept writing, and soon he had a few pages.

For anyone, recounting the hardest period of his or her life would be a difficult undertaking. For Bob, a man with no college education, the task seemed impossible. Soon doubt set in. "After I started writing," he recalls, "I just told myself that I couldn't do it. I thought that, just like everything else in my life, this would fail too."

The truth was that Bob was not a failure; he had been successful at overcoming addiction and maintaining a job. So he turned to the one thing that helped him in the past— prayer. In the next small moment, as the assembly line crept by him, he got on his knees and asked God for help, just like he had done during his recovery. "Something happened," he says. "I was inspired." Bob then finished writing his story in a few days.

The next step for Bob was to actually type the story that he had handwritten while working on the assembly line. With no one to turn to for help with the typing, he figured he would try it himself. The problem, he soon realized, was that he had no computer or typewriter of his own and definitely had no money to buy one.

The resourcefulness that allowed him to find the time to write his story while working led him to find a typewriter in an office where he worked. So, just as he used the small moments while working on the assembly line to write his story, he used his breaks and time after work to type it. He had never learned how to type and never had any experience using a typewriter, but as he sat there in the empty office staring at the letters on the typewriter keys, he started pecking away using one finger to type his story of recovery.

Now, with a finished product in his hands—a very personal account of overcoming addiction—Bob was ready to share it with the world. He thought his story would be best told as a play, a performance in which people would see for themselves what his struggle was like. He had no experience with acting or theatrical productions, but he approached a local theater anyway.

With the same audacity that gave him the courage to write the play while on the assembly line and to sneak into an office at his job to type it, Bob presented that final product to the local theater with the hope that they would let him perform it.

The response he received was a blow to the optimism he had about his idea all along. The local theater immediately rejected his manuscript. "They said 'no way, it's too raw, too real, and not our cup of tea.'" He then presented the idea to a local community college. Their response was the same. Next he tried a different location, another community college, which gave a third, crushing rejection. Now he did not know what to do, and doubt crept in again.

"After I got turned down so many times, I went home and locked myself in my house," he says. "I couldn't understand why it wasn't moving forward."

But Bob had come so far already that he could not give up just yet. The response he had been seeking was actually not too far off. The next day, after a friend convinced him to keep trying, the manuscript that Bob had put so much of himself into was passed along to several friends. One of those friends was involved in an upcoming convention of hospitals and treatment centers and passed the manuscript along to the organizing committee for the event. Bob finally got the news he had been waiting for—the organizing committee wanted Bob's play to be performed at the convention.

Bob's work was finally paying off. But now he had to overcome one more obstacle before he would see his play performed for the first time. "I didn't know any actors or anything about how to direct a play." Fortunately, Bob had never let what he did not know stop him—he never knew how to write a play, but he wrote one—and now he was not going to let the fact that he had never been involved with the production of a theatrical performance stop him. His spirituality led him to believe that if he asked for something and believed it would happen, then he would receive it. So he went to the most generous place he could think of—a church—and he was given space to rehearse the play.

Next he needed a group of actors to comprise the cast of the play. Of course, he did not know any actors, but in the years that he was addicted to drugs and alcohol and during the time he spent in recovery, he had met many individuals like himself who had experienced a broad range of emotions from the worst despair to the greatest joy. So he recruited some of the people he met during his own recovery and then spent the next few months rehearsing with them in the two churches that had graciously obliged his request for rehearsal space.

As soon as Bob felt the group was ready for the first performance at the convention, he thought that it might be good to test the play to see if an audience would see the power that he, himself, saw in it. The best place he thought to test the performance would be a center where the audience would be composed of individuals receiving treatment for addictions. It was at Integrity House, a treatment center in New Jersey, that Bob first saw his play come to life before an audience. It was there that his belief that he was onto something was confirmed.

"When the show was over, a man was weeping about the damage he had done to his son, and several people in the audience came up and hugged us. Then we did another show there that same night, and it was the same reaction. And that reaction continued the next day at the convention."

Since those first performances in 1991, Bob's play, *Visions*, has increased in length from twenty-five minutes to an hour and fifteen minutes. Beginning in New Jersey, the play has now been performed in six states and viewed by over 25,000 people. And the magic that he saw in the first performance is still there today.

"In the play, there are about twenty-two vignettes that depict different scenarios of people trying to overcome addictions," he says. "People always come up to me and say, 'I now understand addiction as a sickness, not a moral relapse.' And they are able to identify with what the struggle is like and, in turn, they see that it's possible for them or their loved ones to recover."

Although some of the original cast members still work with him, he has since had over three hundred volunteer cast members—all of whom have been in recovery at hospitals, treatment centers, or prisons. "They've each added something to it," Bob says. "The majority have had no formal training in acting, but they're good because they've been in the conditions and experienced the things that no actor would ever experience. They're such great performers because they have real emotions—such anger, joy, and despair that a lot of people don't have to live with. A lot of people take for granted things like hugging your family, being able to put food on the table, or greeting your neighbors in the morning, but for recovering people those are gifts that they didn't have before. So they use that, and when we perform, they are out there depicting very hardcore stuff."

Along the journey that has brought *Visions* to different parts of the country, Bob and his cast have tried to remain anonymous despite all the attention such a successful production could bring. "I believe this is a gift, so I kept that and thought I must be humble," Bob explains. "There are no pictures of us, and we hardly ever use full names. For ten years I never asked for a dime. This was funded mostly out of pocket."

Dealing with the expenses of a theatrical production has meant the volunteer cast gets involved in the production as more than just actors. "A lot of the places where we perform, theater groups have never been, and so there are no stages," Bob says. "We have to set those up ourselves. We have to rent trucks, equipment, and do it all ourselves. But it's worth it because we get to go into these hospitals, treatment centers, and prisons and give them a message of hope and inspiration."

The passion that Bob feels for *Visions* and its message of hope is obvious from all that he experienced and overcame to see the play brought to life and performed before thousands of individuals. He says now, "I felt so passionate that this was something inspired by something great that I knew I had to do the foot work. It was very difficult. I didn't know what I was doing, but I knew that it was right. When I walked into the rooms of twelve-step programs when I was at my lowest, it was the recovering alcoholic and drug user that greeted me with kindness and compassion. There were no great speeches or lectures; they just grabbed my hand, patted me on the back, gave me a smile, and just made me feel loved—and I never forgot that. I realized in those great silent acts, God speaks. Even if I had the opportunity, I could never pay that back."

Since those small moments back in 1991 when Bob first started writing *Visions*, he has been able to inspire people dealing with the same struggle that he once faced. And as the director of the play that he typed one finger at a time and that was rejected the first three times he presented it, he is an example of the hope he now shares.

"I can't say that the addicts who watch our show are getting clean and sober because of us, but the joy of getting there, giving them hope, and knowing that we might have made a dent has made it a great journey."

ELISSA MONTANTI
Founder and President
The Global Medical Relief Fund, Inc.

*"All children are equal. No children deserve to have dignity
and youth taken away from them."*

For many people, the strange occurrences that happen throughout life are mere coincidences—meeting someone who helps lead you in a new direction at a time when you are ready to move on, or a phone call that comes just when you need to hear the reassuring voice of a friend. For Elissa Montanti, these occurrences are not just random events to be disregarded, but instead are the work of a higher power that can lead you on a journey to finding your true purpose. Elissa's journey began with a letter that changed her life and the lives of many children around the world.

When Bosnia and the surrounding area were at the forefront of the news, Elissa looked for a way she could get involved in helping the children there. She attended a fundraiser in New York that would provide toys and school supplies for Bosnian children. As the event came to an end, the fundraiser was over—but Elissa was just getting started.

Although their contributions and attendance at this event gave many of the guests a feeling of satisfaction that they had done their part to help, Elissa could not just walk away. She wanted to do more for the children who were the focus of the evening, but she did not know where to start. She had done her share of volunteering and had been an inspiration to those around her as a poet and musician, but now she wanted to do more. She just did not know what there was to be done. What could she do to help children in a foreign country going through horrible circumstances? How could she possibly make a difference in their lives? These questions would soon be answered.

Before she left the fundraiser that day, she was introduced to a diplomat from the United Nations. She asked him her burning question—how could she help? "These children need more than toys and school supplies," the diplomat responded. This response was fuel to the fire she had to make a positive difference in the children's lives.

When she left the event that day, she knew this would be more than just a one-time volunteering experience. Still, she was not sure what exactly she could do. She made an appointment to visit the diplomat who had validated her desire to do more. During their meeting she posed the same question: "What can I do to help?" This time, he handed her a letter.

As Elissa read the letter, she could hear the writer's voice speaking directly to her. It was from a young boy in Bosnia named Kenan. He wrote of his encounter with a landmine— how he had stepped on it and lost both of his arms and a leg. Then she noticed the pictures that were included with the letter, pictures that showed the result of the landmine explosion. After reading his letter and seeing the pictures, her next steps were clear. It was no longer a mystery to her how she could help these children.

Over the next few weeks, Elissa made it her mission to find a way to get Kenan the medical help he needed. Constantly in contact with airlines and hospitals, she used her desire to help, along with the strong emotions she experienced from Kenan's letter and pictures, to convince companies and organizations to make it possible for Kenan to come to the United States and receive prosthetic limbs.

Within a month of reading the letter, Elissa managed to get Kenan and his mother to the United States for the medical attention that he could not receive at home. For the next three months, Kenan and his mother lived with her. Elissa soon learned that the letter she read was not the first time Kenan had asked for help. Actually, he had written many letters, but no one responded. Looking back on her experience helping Kenan, Elissa says, "It was as if the letter was meant for me to read. I believe it was, because it changed my life."

After getting Kenan the help he needed, including prosthetic limbs that now give him full functionality, Elissa knew she could not stop there. She had already gone beyond what anyone could have asked of her. But after her success in pulling together a coalition of hospitals, airlines, and prosthetic device companies to give a young boy from Bosnia the chance to walk again, she knew that there had to be more children whom she could help.

Elissa set her sights on finding the next child to help. It would not be as simple as having a letter handed to her. This time she would need to raise funds to travel to Bosnia herself in order to get a first-hand look at what the children in orphanages and hospitals were facing.

Bosnia was a great distance from her hometown of New York City, but it was close to her heart and where she could take her next step. From this trip and the children she helped, Elissa knew she was changing the lives of the children as well as her own. This success and her newfound calling led her to create the Global Medical Relief Fund, which provides a permanent mechanism for providing prosthetic devices for children wounded in war-torn countries.

Since founding the organization, Elissa has provided prosthetics for children in countries such as Pakistan, Niger, Sierra Leone, and Mexico. Elissa receives many requests from, and has visited, Iraq. With the tense situation there, her work has more recently involved battles just to get visas for the children to come to the United States to receive prosthetics.

One recent example during her last visit to the region involved a five-year-old girl whom Elissa was determined to help. This girl had not only lost a leg, but she also lost her brother and her home as a result of a missile attack. Although she could not give the girl back the life she had known, Elissa was determined to at least give her the chance to walk again. But there was an obstacle in her way.

"This girl lost everything, and they denied her father a visa," Elissa says. "We advocated for them, but they didn't want to hear anything."

Elissa's unyielding determination had always pulled her through, even when overcoming seemingly impossible missions such as this. She had always been able to get a visa. "If you back down, you won't get it," she says. "There's no reason that these children shouldn't be able to get a new leg, especially since their parents are gentle and wonderful."

This five-year-old girl and her father were eventually able to get a visa, and the girl has visited Elissa in the United States twice since receiving a prosthetic leg.

Most of the children who come to the United States to receive prosthetics through Elissa's organization change as much on the inside as they do on the outside. "They come here very shy, especially the kids from Iraq," Elissa observes. "They've been through horrible experiences. There's a sadness within them that no other child has, and some of them are scared. But give them not even a day and you can see them change." And over the weeks or months that they stay here, their bond with Elissa grows strong.

When reflecting on the hard times she has had with the work she does, Elissa says, "I have strong, quiet faith. Sometimes I don't have money to bring the next child and don't know where I'll get the money, but every time I thought I couldn't do it there was a grant or a donation that came through. There's a sense of reward for all you go through. When you see a child walk who had to be in a wheelchair on the airplane, that's what it's all about.

"I could have given up a long time ago, but I never did. I truly believe that determination is the key to success in anything. A lot of people ask why I spend my own money doing this, but I just went with my heart. What I do is because I didn't think logically—if I thought logically, I never would have gotten where I am."

It is her heart that supports the work she does and earns her praise for the children's lives that she has changed. What started out as just her desire to help has placed her in *The New York Times*, *People* magazine, and on the *Dr. Phil Show*.

Elissa's work and her organization have grown since the first child she helped came to the United States. As the organization grows to helping almost twenty children each year, she still keeps the personal touch. "The uniqueness of the charity is that it's small," she says. "Wanting it to grow to a hundred kids each year is good, but if that happens, I still want to be involved with the kids and the families. Maybe I won't have to clean the sheets and make the beds, but I still want to be involved personally."

Things have definitely changed for Elissa since she attended that first fundraiser in New York for Bosnian children. One thing that has not changed is her desire to help. Even after providing prosthetic limbs to Kenan, she has continued to be there for him. Today, Kenan helps Elissa with the work of her organization. She says, "He is an inspiration to the charity. The children look at him and think, if he lost two arms and a leg and could get better, they can do it too."

TOM PRICHARD
Founder and Executive Director
Sudan Sunrise, Inc.

"There is a dawn coming that has the potential to radically change things—we want to help that change happen."

In 2004, when Tom Prichard began to hear news about genocide in the Darfur region of Sudan, what he saw was more than just another news story. As the mission pastor for Christ Church, Anglican in Overland Park, Kansas, he just could not turn away from the news of brutal violence and genocide. For so many people who see tragic stories on television or read about them in newspapers, it can be easy to feel overwhelmed and powerless. For Tom, having spent much of his life organizing mission work, he knew there had to be something he could do to have an impact on what was going on in Sudan.

To gain a better understanding of the conflict in Sudan and to learn what could be done, Tom turned to a Sudanese friend in Kansas. He was completely astonished by the friend's response to his questions. "The Darfurians deserve what is happening to them," the friend said. "Muslims from Dafur killed many of my family and helped kill over two million southern Sudanese."

This was not the response Tom had expected. For this friend, and many others, the history of conflict in Sudan was a bitter reality that had often gone unreported in the news. The friend was from southern Sudan, a region where many individuals were killed by the Sudanese government army, which used the Muslims from Darfur to support its attacks.

Despite Sudan's unfortunate past, Tom remained focused on finding a way to help the current conflict. "As I continued to watch the news about Darfur," he says, "I was deeply troubled. As a Christian I thought I needed to do what I could to help the southern Sudanese not just forgive the Darfurians but to also come to their aid."

Tom continued his search for a way he could help ease the tension in Sudan. "This idea wouldn't go away. I knew this was the moment that there could be a breakthrough in reconciliation in Sudan if the southerners would come to the rescue of their former persecutors." To some it was a radical proposal—that former victims of the Dafurians would now come to their aid—but for Tom, it was a great place to start.

Tom took his idea, along with a few questions, to the executive director of the Sudan Council of Churches USA, who told him that when he was a child, Darfurian soldiers killed his mother and father. The director told Tom, "We just had a meeting of our executive committee, and we decided unanimously that the SCC-USA will do all it can to help the people of Darfur. We know what they are going through, because the same thing was done to us. As Christians we have to forgive them and help them in their moment of need."

What Tom heard that day was enough to propel him to action. His response to the powerful expression of forgiveness he had just heard was, "It is clear that God is putting something together, and we have to do something."

That something they decided to do was to send an exploratory team to Chad—a neighboring country of Sudan—to get a first-hand account of what was going on in the region.

The team that was sent included three Sudanese and one American. Although Tom did not travel with that team, he was the main organizer for the first and subsequent relief missions. The first challenge for the team to overcome was finding exactly where to go once they arrived and who they should talk to. Although they followed several leads from contacts they had in the United States and in Sudan, the group was unable to find the connection they sought. Even though their leads were unsuccessful, the team decided they would travel to Chad anyway and take with them their strong faith that they would be led to the right people.

Upon leaving the United States with no idea whom they should talk to or how they would exactly help once they arrived, this exploratory team began their trip. While changing planes in Paris, they came across a man from Chad. When asked what kind of work he did there, he informed them that he worked for the government of Chad as the main coordinator between the government, humanitarian organizations, and the United Nations for the benefit of Darfurian refugees. Unbelievably, the group had found the exact connection they had been looking for even before they arrived in the country.

When they arrived in Chad, other doors opened, and the team was able to visit two refugee camps at the Sudan border. Although they had good intentions, their arrival was met with hostility. That tension, however, slowly began to unwind. After talking to some of the individuals in the camp and relaying their reason for being there, the exploratory team heard something that validated their purpose. One of the men they met in the camp of Dafurian refugees shared his story of being involved in the killing of southern Sudanese. With tears in his eyes he said, "We raped women, we burned villages, and tied men and boys as if they were animals. At night we killed them and left their bodies for hyenas to eat. Please forgive me for what I have done. May God have mercy on me."

The expression from this man and others in the camps they visited highlighted the possibility of reconciliation among the Sudanese people. When they learned two weeks later that Sudan's leader, Omar Al-Bashir, had spoken out against them, the team knew they were onto something groundbreaking.

During their brief stay in Chad, the team received an urgent appeal for clothing from Darfurian refugee leaders, urging the team to come to their aid. They knew that before they could start on reconciliation, they had to address some of the immediate needs of the refugees. Back in the United States, Tom and the other interested individuals began collecting clothes to send to the Darfurian refugees in Chad. After collecting over fifty pallets of clothing and receiving a donation of 25,000 pounds of powdered milk, there was a problem—their expected providers of air freight all fell through.

With all of the donated items just sitting there, something had to be done. When a shipping company was contacted, it was determined that to ship all they had collected would cost $150,000. After attempting to raise the money, only $50,000 had been received. Knowing that the lives of the Sudanese refugees hung in the balance, Tom paid the remaining amount of $100,000. It was definitely a leap of faith for a clergyman living a modest lifestyle.

When the shipment arrived in Chad, a Sudanese Muslim leader expressed his gratitude to the exploratory team and asked for forgiveness. "We killed you for twenty years, please forgive us," he said. "We ask you to stand with us now, so we may have peace like you have peace in the south," he said.

There could not have been a clearer sign to Tom that it was time to spread that message. "We realized that the United Nations was taking care of the emergency needs in Darfur, so we decided to get the message of forgiveness out to the southern Sudanese."

Tom's life soon became consumed with doing just that. "We distributed thousands of these messages asking the southern Sudanese to forgive Darfurians. As our activities grew, it became clear to me that I needed to do this full-time."

In November 2005, Tom left his job as mission pastor of his church to start Sudan Sunrise, an organization committed to encouraging reconciliation between the Darfurian Muslims and the southern Sudanese Christians. "This is a moment when there can be a huge reconciliation in Sudan among Christians and Muslims," he said at the time.

One of the challenges faced by Sudan Sunrise is that the southern Sudanese are often excluded when groups demonstrate for an end of the genocide in Darfur. "Many activists don't want to include the southern Sudanese. Perhaps they fear that Americans won't want to help if people learn that many Darfurians were used to kill southern Sudanese, so some people want to keep that side of the story quiet."

But what some people see as a past that should not be discussed, Tom sees as a potential catalyst for change. "It seems to me that there is a moment for a breakthrough, which I would compare to when the Berlin Wall came down. Some people never believed that the wall would come down peacefully. Today if the equivalent of the Berlin Wall ran through Sudan, it would be a bloody wall. The way to tear down this wall is to build relationships. We find so many southern Sudanese who want to help Darfurians—we just need to multiply that about 100,000 times."

Reflecting on his journey that started in Kansas and now reaches to the heart of Sudan, Tom says, "I've been involved in things related to Christian missions for twenty-five years. With the work we've done there is no other explanation other than that God is at work causing some breakthroughs. We have a little tiny effort, but it was significant enough for the dictator of Sudan to speak against us. When the story is said and done, our little bit may be invisible, but if we help encourage, push, and nudge things along, if we can just help, that would be fine."

EMMA RHODES, ED.D.
Founder
The Emma Rhodes Education and Multipurpose Center

"People see me and say, 'If you can do it, so can I,'
and I am there to tell them yes, yes they can."

Sitting behind a desk, Dr. Emma Kelly Rhodes waited for another person to walk in. It would not be long before the next person would pass through the entrance, see her, and ask in disbelief, "You're a doctor?" Her response: "Yes, but I'm not a medical doctor. I have a doctorate in education."

This was not the first time she had been asked this question, and it definitely would not be the last. The disbelief is understandable—it is not often that someone walking into a laundromat to wash clothes sees a woman seated behind a desk with a nameplate with the title "Dr." But for the residents of one of Little Rock, Arkansas' forgotten communities, it would become a familiar sight.

"I'm Dr. Emma Kelly Rhodes. How are you?" And from that point on, she would have the full attention and awe of the person that, just moments ago, met her presence with disbelief. It is easy to see why such a sight would seem so strange. Here, in a community where reaching your high school graduation is a feat and college may as well be light years away—an unreachable place that is more fiction than reality—it is difficult to comprehend why such an educated woman would spend parts of her days sitting behind a desk in a laundromat. But for Dr. Rhodes, it made perfect sense. If she did not spend time there, who else would be there to serve as an example of what determination, tenacity, and faith can do? Who else would create a place where anyone could come, irrespective of their past and lack of education, to receive tutoring, find a job, or just to get some hope from a seemingly endless source? It made perfect sense—it had to be her.

From a young age, Emma understood the importance of having someone to turn to for help and inspiration. She was once in need of both. At age fifteen, she had to face the unfortunate reality of being a high school dropout—not because she was not interested in education, but because she became pregnant. Being pregnant at that time meant you could not attend school. So she left, but against her will. Although some may have been delighted to no longer have to attend school, for Emma it was hard to leave her education behind. It was her dream to become a schoolteacher, and having to leave only meant her dream moved further away. But with that dream now pushed away, she turned to another source of comfort—her family.

It was the 1950s. In College Station, Arkansas, as in other parts of the country, the rules of culture and society did not look favorably upon unwed mothers. So she married at the age of fifteen and became engrossed in the life of being a mother and a wife. Over the next several years, she gave birth to a child at ages seventeen, eighteen, twenty-one, and twenty-four.

Although she had her hands full with obligations to her family as a mother, as well as having dropped out of school ten years earlier, Emma still had a desire to be a teacher. But in order to do so, she would need to complete the education that she had been shut out from ten years before. So at the age of twenty-five she began again.

"One day I heard about the GED program," she says, "and I thought here is my opportunity to get my diploma. Being a mother and being married hadn't ended my desire to learn. So I did it."

After that she had two more children. And by the age of twenty-nine, she had all that she ever wanted. She had a husband, seven children, and a GED that would help her achieve her dream of being a schoolteacher. Then the life that she had known took a dramatic turn—her husband died from cancer, leaving Emma to be a single parent to seven children in 1968 in the south end of Little Rock. There was no choice for her as to whether she would sit in despair with her children, longing for her husband to come back. She knew that the only way she could survive and provide a decent life for her children would be to get a college degree so that she could get a job that would pay her enough to take care of her children.

After taking two weeks to grieve the loss of her husband, Emma enrolled in classes at Philander Smith College. She was able to secure a job as a secretary at the college. Working full-time during the day and taking classes at night, she spent every moment of her life from 1968 until 1972 knowing that the hard work would pay off—and it did. In June 1972 it happened—she received a college degree. But it was not just for her.

"When I got the degree, my children said, 'We got a degree,' because they were so much a part of everything," Emma recalls. "It was really a family effort."

While for Emma, receiving a college degree was an amazing achievement, her mother had bigger plans for her. "After I got the degree, my mother said, 'Listen, baby, is there another degree you can get?' I said, 'Yes, Mama, there's a degree called a master's degree.' My mother said, 'Get it.' I told her that I didn't need a master's to teach school, but she said get it and so I did." Soon after that, she met and married Clyde Rhodes in August 1975.

"After I got the master's degree in 1976 my mother asked if there was another degree I could get," Emma remembers. "I told her that there was one called a specialist's degree. She asked what it was, and I told her it was the degree between a master's and a doctorate. She said, 'Get it.' After I got that she asked again if there was another degree I could get. I said, 'Yes, the highest one you can get is the doctorate.' My mother said, 'Get it.' I asked her why would I need it. She said, 'Listen, baby, it's better to have it and not need it than to need it and not have it—get it.' So I did."

For the next twenty-six years, Dr. Rhodes worked at the Arkansas Department of Education as a job skills and vocational education trainer, eventually serving as the statewide administrator for Arkansas' GED program—the same program that she went through to obtain a GED. In 1998, when she retired, her life was undoubtedly a success, but she still wanted to do more. Sure, she had accomplished more than she or anyone else would have ever imagined possible, but she knew that was not enough. She knew that her achievements and success would mean nothing if she could not share them with others.

To share the knowledge she received, and the wisdom that came with it, she went back to her lifelong dream of being a teacher—but not in the traditional sense. She decided to start by using her experience as a state administrator to tutor adults in the GED program. However, she especially wanted to tutor in an area that was often overlooked and underserved. This way she could be an example and show people from backgrounds similar to hers that they could also succeed.

To start the tutoring, she found a laundromat in an area of Little Rock with high crime rates, drugs, and prostitution. Using the money from her retirement, she acquired the building containing the laundromat, vowing to transform it and the surrounding community. For the first year that she tutored in the building, she sat behind a desk in the laundromat with her nameplate displayed proudly on it. Surrounding her on the walls were plaques from the many awards and honors she had received in addition to pictures of her with political leaders.

Her aim in having this display was not to boast of herself, but to show what is possible.

"All of these things I use now to encourage people. They walk in and ask about them, and I tell them my story and all that I've done. Then they look at me and tell me, 'If you can do it, so can I,' and I am there to tell them yes. Yes, I did it when people said it couldn't be done, and so can you."

For Dr. Rhodes, giving people a chance to succeed means more than giving them hope and inspiration. It means eliminating the conditions that hold their community back. During her first year in the building she came to know the community very well. With the large amount of time she spent in the laundromat tutoring, she befriended many individuals from the community, and in her travels between her home and the laundromat she became observant of the pervasive drug activity. She was so aware of the happenings in the community that she even learned of a location where drug deals were often made. She soon took action.

"There was a place on the corner where they would make drug deals," Dr. Rhodes says. "One day it was placed on my heart to go and anoint the ground where the deals were made. I bought a quart of olive oil, prayed over it, and spread it on the corner and all around the building. I prayed that the criminal activity would go sour, and it has."

From then on she had no doubt that she was meant to be doing this work in that community. And she continued her crusade by talking to as many people in the community as possible. "I went around and asked what kind of services they needed," she says. "I listened and said I would try to meet every need I could." And that is exactly what she has done.

After spending that initial year behind the desk in the laundromat, Dr. Rhodes built on her desire to become a teacher by creating the Emma Rhodes Education and Multipurpose Center. This center, housed in a separate part of the laundromat building, offers classes for adults in the areas of life skills, computer literacy, and, of course, GED programs.

From her many conversations with residents of the neighborhood, she saw even more ways that she could help the community. One such need she met was creating a business center for the neighborhood. At this center, individuals from the community can pay utility bills, make copies, send faxes, and purchase money orders and stamps—all services that were unavailable to the neighborhood before Dr. Rhodes arrived.

Despite her success with the business and adult education center, Dr. Rhodes continued to look for more ways to help. One way actually found her. In December 2003, she faced the violence that she had tried to stop head on. That month, her oldest son was killed—for $95. "I know that the murderer wouldn't have killed my son had he not been hyped up on drugs," she says now. "If he gets out of prison, where is he going to work, who is going to hire him?" This unfortunate circumstance and these subsequent questions led her to start a program to help released offenders find employment.

Now that Dr. Rhodes' center has completely filled the building, she's looking to expand into another facility. Next to her center was an empty house. Today that building represents a vision that she has brought to reality. Offering services including health screenings, job placement, and a clothes closet to provide suitable attire for those obtaining jobs for the first time, this new building is appropriately called the House of Vision. In addition, she is donating office space in the building to a local Stop the Killing campaign, with all these expenses being met by her retirement income.

In describing how she has been able to connect with the community and make an impact on the people there, Dr. Rhodes simply says, "Not only was I able to make friends with them, I was able to identify with them because I was a high school dropout and a single mother. I can identify with them and tell them just because you're there, you don't have to stay there. I think about where I would have been had I not had a family to tell me I could make it despite where I was in life. I'm here saying the same thing to them—if I can make it so can you. I tell people from the White House to the poor house about my struggle and where I come from—and I've been in both."

JOHANA SCOT
Founder and Executive Director
Parent Guidance Center, Inc.

"Help a parent and you've already helped the child."

When Johana Scot began volunteering as a court-appointed special advocate for abused and neglected children in Montgomery County, Texas, she had no idea how much the experience would change her life. Like many of the other volunteers, she had a strong commitment to helping children in need. As a mother of two children, she wanted to give back to children in her community who were not as fortunate as her own.

Johana began the volunteer training program with high hopes for helping to advocate for the children and making a difference in their lives and futures. Maybe if she tried hard enough, she could get a child out of an abusive environment and into a loving home. Maybe if she put forth her best effort, she could help change the system that so often had failed many it sought to protect. Bringing change to the system was exactly what she did, but not as she originally planned.

It seemed quite strange to Johana, during her volunteer training, how the parents of the children were characterized. "It stood out to me and made me uncomfortable the way they talked about the parents," she says. "It was just something I stuck in the back of my mind." But it did not stay in the back of her mind for long.

When she received her first case and began attending court hearings and other appointments as the child advocate, Johana saw more examples of how parents were being disregarded and dismissed from the lives of their children without being afforded even the most basic dignity and respect.

To be fair, Johana was well aware of why many of these parents found themselves in these situations. Some had indeed abused their children, but most of them—including Johana's cases—were not abusive parents. They faced the threat of having their children taken away from them because they were unable to provide basic necessities.

While the other child advocates, case workers, and attorneys involved in these cases saw parents as the enemy and as an evil menace depriving children of healthy lives, Johana saw something different. "I saw parents who had been abused when they were children and were just repeating it or less affluent people who just needed help. So I tried to work with the parents in addition to working with the children."

From that point on she made a concerted effort in all of her cases to work with the parents to find ways that they could get back on their feet and provide an adequate home for their children. But in a system that had for so long viewed the parent as the enemy and not as a person needing help, Johana found it difficult to overcome that false perception. Like the many other volunteers, though, she had a considerable amount of freedom with her cases. For Johana, this meant she had the latitude to work more closely with the parents in her cases.

Reaching out to the parents required a certain amount of empathy and tenacity. Johana was at a loss for neither. Unlike her fellow volunteers, her work held personal significance deeply rooted in her past. As someone who had experienced personal struggles as a single parent, she was able to bring a different perspective.

She recalls, "They have this series of training sessions that you have to go through as a volunteer, but they don't prepare you for what you will see in these cases—they don't train you in poverty or in domestic violence." Johana did not need training in those areas; her life had prepared her for it.

"I would see other people make huge mistakes in their cases because they could not relate," Johana says. "I just didn't fit in with that." One of those mistakes she often saw occurred in the courtroom during hearings. "In court they would sit an abused woman together with the man who abused her, and they would wonder why the woman was lying in court saying he hadn't hurt her. It's because she was afraid. Things like that were popping up everywhere."

What began as a simple attempt to find resources for the parents soon proved to be much more difficult than she had expected. "I couldn't find any helpful information, and I felt hopeless that there was nothing for these parents to help them get better so they could get their children back," she says. The hopelessness that she felt, however, soon fueled her determination to demonstrate to other people what she had long ago recognized—taking a child away from a parent and then not doing anything to help the parent get better was not the best thing for the child.

In the first two cases she was assigned she not only advocated for the child, but she also worked with the parents to get them what they needed to become better parents and keep their family together. After getting the children back with their parents in her first two cases, she felt that she had to do more to change the system. "I figured I needed to start my own organization and wondered how hard it would be to have an organization helping parents become better parents," Johana says.

After countless hours of research with the help of her sister to find information, she found very little. Describing her next steps, Johana recalls, "We began to ask questions. Why is the system this way? Why don't people want to help the parents?" None of the answers she found satisfied her. No one was able to convince her that the way the system worked was the best possible way of bringing families back together.

Sometimes things just seem to fall into place at just the right time. April 2004 was that time for Johana. At that time, Carole Keeton Strayhorn, then the Texas Comptroller, released a report detailing many problems and possible solutions for the Texas foster care system. Titled *Forgotten Children: A Special Report on the Texas Foster Care System*, the report made clear the need for a change in how the state handled foster children. For Johana, it provided the perfect opportunity to present her own solution: the Parent Guidance Center.

Launched as a resource for parents who faced having their parental rights terminated, the Parent Guidance Center began by providing advocacy and parenting classes. Though the program started small, helping only a few parents, Johana still had to face much resistance to the work she was doing. "When you tell people what you do, they assume you are helping abusive and neglectful parents and that they are bad people. So we have to change people's minds."

If changing people's minds is a skill, Johana should be considered a master. The fiery passion and persistence that got her this far was only beginning to warm up. "My response was to try to explain what was really going on. The kids were usually taken for neglect, not abuse. Most of those cases were caused by poverty. The parents were not hurting the kids, they were just single parents with no child support trying to do the best they could."

But changing people's perceptions was not even the most difficult part of opening her own resource center for parents. To be able to guide and advocate for parents on how to be better equipped to handle parenthood, Johana would need much more training and education. After more rounds of research with the help of her sister, she came across what seemed to be the perfect fit for her organization.

Developed by Dr. Stephen Bavolek, a recognized leader in the field of parenting education, the Nurturing Parenting Program is used to teach effective parenting strategies including the prevention and treatment of child abuse and neglect. Having found this program, next on the list for Johana was to get trained as a facilitator and to advertise for the parenting classes that her organization would provide.

To try to have an immediate impact on the families that she saw in the system she wanted to change, she began offering classes only for those parents who were already in the process of having their parental rights terminated. She even reached out to other organizations that worked with clients in the child welfare system. What seemed like a great idea to Johana did not seem so to others.

"The resistance we were met with from other organizations was mostly about funding," she says. "They didn't care what we were doing they just didn't want us to take grant money away from them." But money was never an issue for Johana and the Parent Guidance Center. Making money and winning grants were secondary to providing a much-needed service. In fact, she believed so much in her idea that she used her own money to bring it to life. Her response to these critics was always the same, "We're self-funded, and we're helping people and going in debt to do it."

To make a dent in the system that she thought was in need of repair, Johana stayed motivated by reminding herself and those around her of the situation facing many of the parents. "Parents are set up for failure by the system because of all the appointments they have to attend," she says. "They have to go to court visits, go to various counseling sessions, and keep a job. No one can keep a job under these conditions, especially when you're in a minimum wage position. The system doesn't understand that, so we have to bring them back to reality."

Despite providing a variety of services and workshops for parents, Johana believes that the best service they provide is hope. "We give them hope," she says. "That's what they need. They will give up if they don't have it." This hope does not just come from teaching them to be better parents. It also comes from the personal touch that Johana gives each parent. Not only does she spend up to eighteen months attending court hearings and working on the case with them, but they often eat together and even cry together. This is why she feels such a personal connection to the parents—she knows so much more than just what is presented on paper to the court.

Providing this kind of personal service sometimes means she is unable to serve every possible client, but that does not stop her. Now that she has been working with parents and the Parent Guidance Center for a few years, she has become known for what she does. Though it might appear that most of her work is advocacy, empowering is how she likes to think of it.

"We don't ever make a recommendation to the court on whether the kid should go home," she says. "The purpose is to equip the parent. Parents don't come to us if they don't really want help. If parents say they want help, they have to show me that they are serious about changing. I turn them into people that can take care of the kids. If the parent is not willing to do that, then he or she won't be our client. These parents are motivated to get their children home; they just don't know how to do it."

The success of Johana's organization is clear—since the beginning, there has only been one client of hers that has had parental rights terminated. Johana attributes that one dark instance to the parent's lack of transportation and not being able to get to an appointment. "It wasn't because she didn't love her kid; it was because she didn't have a car to get to the numerous appointments." But just like before, this one failure only gave Johana even more reason to continue.

While her frustration with the system gives her the motivation to dedicate her life to keeping families together, her compassion and love for children shows as well. For many children a teddy bear can be just a toy or a simple bedroom decoration. For the children of the parents Johana helps, however, it means so much more. "Many of the children are separated from their parents for so long they fear that they will forget what their parents look like," she says. So in addition to getting a friend who gives them hope, children can also receive a small teddy bear with a picture of their parents attached to it.

When asked why she gives so much of her time and money to this cause, Johana responds, "I'm compelled to do this work because I believe you are responsible to fix what you know is wrong. So many people told me I couldn't change the system, but I didn't listen to them." Describing a specific instance, she says, "When I first starting working on creating the Parent Guidance Center, my supervisor at the court-appointed special advocate program told me, 'Johana, you can't change the system.'" Johana responded at the time, "You watch me." Several months later, after she had some success with the Parent Guidance Center, Johana went back to her former supervisor, handed her a business card, and told her, "Oh yeah, yes I can."

And every day she lives by that idea. "We're not satisfied changing the system case-by-case, we want to change the system." With this in mind, Johana now spends much of her time at the state capital in Austin, Texas, advocating for a better child welfare system that protects the children and empowers the parents to be better parents. "Tell me that I didn't change the system," she says. "Tell me that one little person with passion and no money can't change the system. I won't believe it."

ROBINA SUWOL
Founder and Executive Director
California Safe Schools, Inc.

*"If you speak from the heart and come from a place
of really wanting to do good, people will listen."*

It began as an ordinary day for Robina. She ushered her two sons into the car to drive them to school like so many times before. Although she had done this before, she still took great care in simple things, such as giving them healthy food in the mornings and driving carefully so they would arrive safely at school. For her, their school was also a safe haven—a place where they would be immune from danger and where hazards could not reach them. On this day, however, that peace of mind she had in dropping her two sons off at school would change right in front of her.

As they reached the school and pulled up to the curb, her two children got out of the car and ran toward the school to meet their friends. Before driving away, Robina waited for her sons to look back at her so she could blow them a kiss. But her youngest son turned around to look back at her and instead of smiling he shouted, "It tastes terrible, Mommy."

Robina noticed a man standing nearby wearing a white uniform similar to those worn by law enforcement officials when handling hazardous materials. The man in this suit was spraying what appeared to be a mist in the front of the school steps and entrance. "I thought he might be prepping the rails in front of the school to be painted," she says. But for her son, who had a history of asthma, even such a seemingly minor substance had the potential for bringing back unpleasant symptoms.

Concerned about her son's asthma, she immediately called the school to find out what was being sprayed near the children as they entered the school building. What she learned from that telephone call disturbed her. "I called the school office and found out that at that time there was no requirement for school districts to notify the school site if work was being performed around the school," she says. "They advised me to call their district office downtown. Initially they were reluctant to tell me the name of the product, which I desperately needed to know in case an antidote was required. So I kept talking to them on the phone and mentioned that the yard looked beautiful. It was then that they told me the name of the chemical. It was not a product that could be purchased off a store shelf. What I found out about this product on the Internet led me to believe that it should not be used around children, animals, or really anyone because it had a significant number of health risks."

When Robina went back to the school to pick up her children, she found that her youngest son had become ill. "He was wheezing and scared. He asked me if this was going to happen to him again, or to his friends. Without hesitation but with no plan, I comforted him by saying, 'No, of course not.' I realized how fortunate I was that I witnessed the chemical assault. But I thought, what about parents who aren't at school to see chemicals being sprayed? Children might get sick, and a parent wouldn't know the source. It haunted me, and I thought something needed to be done."

From there Robina sprang into action, researching alternatives to pesticides and compiling medical and scientific research to help convince the school district to end the use of harmful pesticides. Her passion for ensuring that schools are healthy places for children led her to create an non-profit organization.

This children's environmental health coalition that she created—California Safe Schools—would become the mechanism through which she would mobilize concerned parents, teachers, medical experts, and community members to bring a change to the practice of using potentially harmful pesticides.

For one year, California Safe Schools met with the Los Angeles Unified School District (LAUSD) to create a groundbreaking policy. Results finally emerged exactly one year after Robina witnessed the pesticide use at her son's school, and everyone took notice.

This group devised a policy that would guide the LAUSD along a path of ensuring that any chemicals used at schools had been proven to be safe for use around children. The policy, known as Integrated Pest Management, required training for school staff and contractors on the use and risk of chemicals. Since the time this policy was adopted by the school district, it has become a national and international model as a way to ensure the safety of children from hazardous chemicals. In addition, the policy included a rule requiring schools to provide a list to parents of the chemicals that will be used at the school.

Robina attributes the success of the policy to its approach. "This policy embraces the precautionary principle and includes parents' right to know about chemicals used at schools. 'Be safe, not sorry' is the theme of the policy."

When Integrated Pest Management was adopted in 1999, the number of products that could be used in the school district dropped from 136 products to 36 low-risk products. The success of this policy led to the California Healthy Schools Act of 2000.

To ensure implementation of the newly created policy, Robina and California Safe Schools worked with an LAUSD board member to form an oversight committee. For the past several years, a 15-member committee has met monthly. Robina has not missed a single meeting.

It was at one of these meetings that Robina found the next challenge for her and California Safe Schools to take on. "We often have guest speakers," she says. "At one meeting a speaker came specifically to request that some of our schools be used to test experimental pesticides with unknown side effects. The speaker promoted the experimental product as safer because it is stronger, thereby requiring less of the product to be used. The oversight team, comprised of scientists, medical experts, parents, environmentalists, and district staff, emphatically declined the offer. As the speaker departed, his final comment was, 'That's ok, if LA Unified doesn't want to use it, I have other school districts lined up.' That comment—that K-12 public schools could be used to test chemical products—haunted me."

For Robina, that meant she had to do something about it. "I told this story at an event, and a staff person of a member of the California Assembly was present. They relayed the story, and the assembly member agreed to author a bill to ban this kind of testing."

In October 2006, the bill was sponsored by California Safe Schools and signed by the governor. Today, more than six million school children, along with hundreds of thousands of teachers and school employees, are protected from experimental pesticides whose health effects are unknown. Additionally, the law prohibits the practice of continuing the use of phased-out pesticides on school sites.

Reflecting on the challenges she faced in her work through California Safe Schools, Robina says, "I believe when we work together great things can happen. Our children are not lab rats. I believe there is a tremendous need to recognize the relationship between health and our environment. California Safe Schools enjoys sharing resources and is committed to helping others create safer environments for the most vulnerable—our children. This is especially important when you consider that chemical exposure thresholds are based on a 160-pound healthy adult male."

Described as a good organizer and tireless when it comes to something she really cares about, Robina used the concern that she had the day she started her mission to bring change to a system that had, until then, resisted it. "I had to show that I wasn't just a mommy tree-hugger coming in to create problems," she says. "I wanted to help. I realized that every day the policy was not in place was a day that a child could potentially become ill. I didn't want to worry about kids and wonder what others were going to spray the next day."

Robina's persistence, tempered with just the right amount of politeness, transformed one parent's concern into California Safe Schools and two policies that have changed the way California's school districts use pesticides. Today Robina still holds onto her goal of providing a safe environment for children.

SOPHIA KEY WEST
Founder and Executive Director
Mothers Against Predators

"Just because you've been victimized you don't need to dwell in victim mentality. If you channel your energies to help others rise above atrocities, you become victorious."

On a typical day, Sophia Key West's life is set in a fairy tale. Adorned in elegant attire and a crown befitting a queen, she stands surrounded by a castle that provides refuge and power to those who visit it. While there, she displays various illusions with the wave of her wand, and those who look on receive more than just a treat for their eyes—they receive a strength that empowers them to defend against the predators that lie beyond the castle walls.

As magical as it may seem, this castle is not in some faraway land. It is in Beltsville, Maryland, and is home to the Good Knight Child Empowerment Network. Founded in 1985 by retired federal law enforcement agents, the network has made its primary mission the goal of preventing children from falling prey to sexual predators. Leading the cause was Edward Jagen, who wanted to find a creative and imaginative way to teach children how to protect themselves and defend against child predators. This desire to bring creativity to an area of crime prevention led to the storybook, *A Good Knight Story*.

The story follows a medieval hero, the Blue Knight, on a quest to teach children how to protect themselves from the deceptions often used by child predators. Once published, the book was distributed and used by many school districts throughout the country as a method of educating children about how to defend against adults seeking to take advantage of them.

With the success of the book, the Good Knight Network became a national mechanism for getting this type of educational material to children and for increasing the awareness of the threats posed by child predators. The network's main focus is to distribute educational materials to communities and schools to equip as many families as possible with the knowledge needed to keep their children safe. Through a grassroots approach, everyone who participates in the educational program in their community is "knighted" and encouraged to equip ten more individuals with the same information.

This message hit close to home for many parents. For Sophia, it had an even more powerful meaning. As a parent, she wanted to do everything possible to ensure that her own children would not have to live with the horror of being sexually abused. Like most parents, she just wanted the best life possible for her children—a life where they would not have their innocence taken away from them at a young age and where they would not have to deal with such terror for the rest of their lives.

While she wanted what almost any other parent would want for their child, her own experiences provided her with an even stronger motivation to protect her children. It was her own experience of being abused as a child that was pushing her to become an educator and advocate in an effort to prevent others from having to experience the same horror that she did.

After going through a childhood of abuse and dealing with the residual effects that remained into her adult life, Sophia had first-hand experience in knowing what to do to help others protect themselves from abuse. "I would sit my children down and tell them not to go anywhere with strangers," she says.

About the same time as she was teaching her children about being safe, the threat of child abduction and abuse had been brought to the nation's attention with the abduction and murder of a boy in Florida in 1981. This news gave Sophia even more resolve to ensure that the children in her family would never have to face the threat of a child predator. "I thought for sure I had taught them everything they needed to know to be safe," she recalls.

With all that she had taught them and as much as she tried, her confidence that her children would be immune from these threats was shattered. It was on a Christmas Eve that she began to relive the terror of her own childhood when her son attempted suicide. Despite her diligence and best intentions, her son had been molested by his soccer coach, who was also a friend of their family.

It was not a stranger or even a convicted pedophile released from jail, it was a trusted family friend. "It was horrifying to see my son, who was a straight 'A' student and great athlete, go from that to a child whose spirit was tarnished and whose innocence was robbed," she says.

She knew that she had to devote her life to helping other families prevent this same thing from happening to them. "When all this came to light, I said I couldn't let this happen again," she says. "I couldn't let another parent or child feel the way I felt. I couldn't let another parent go through the horror of what I went through."

The first step in her quest led her to the Good Knight Network, where she became a volunteer. The network had recently received land to build a facility where children could learn how to protect themselves from child predators. The facility would not be just a typical community center or classroom; instead, it would be a magical place and home to the Blue Knight. This would be where the Good Knight story would come to life and where children who came would be "knighted" and given the powers of the Blue Knight to protect themselves.

As a volunteer, Sophia became involved in leading some of the programs for children. While her sheer passion and motivation to convey the information to children would be enough, she also brought her own skills as a magician to help convey the information in a creative way.

"When we do programs, they are in a fairy-tale setting. We start off with magic tricks for half an hour or more and then we ask them for another word for 'trick.' When they say it's a deception, I tell them that these are fun deceptions, but that there are also bad deceptions that people may use to take advantage of them. Then we show them a video that highlights the ten basic psychological deceptions that predators use to lure a child away into dangerous situations. We get them to realize that they have the power to say no and the power to tell someone."

Sophia's quest to prevent other families from experiencing the terror that she had experienced grew to an even larger scale recently when she founded Mothers Against Predators as a division of the Good Knight Network. Encouraged by the success of the Good Knight Network's educational materials and outraged by the recurrence of national news stories of child abductions, mothers across the country wanted to band together to reach even more families. Many of the mothers who got involved were also disturbed that the national media only showed the problem that existed but did not provide people with information on how to prevent it.

"It really took off because of the outrage from concerned citizens asking why the media couldn't take this to the next step: education," Sophia says. "You have to take it one step further. So I started Mothers Against Predators. There are thousands of mothers across the country doing the Good Knight program and teaching as many children as they can in a grassroots effort to blanket our nation's children with awareness."

Sophia's work through Mothers Against Predators still allows her to don her crown and perform illusions for children, but now she does it on a much larger scale. Through educating groups of children and their parents on how to defend against predators, she reaches about 30,000 families each year. She often travels to different cities to conduct the programs and has even presented the program to 20,000 children and parents in the Houston Astrodome at one time.

"When you look out at an audience knowing that the U.S. Department of Justice estimates that seven out of ten girls and three out of seven boys will be victimized before their eighteenth birthday and you see such a large audience of mostly children, you know you are reaching a large mass of kids who have the possibility of becoming victims. There's really nothing greater than knowing that I am reaching these kids. I hope that I can reach just one that won't have to go through what I went through."

The results of her work are undisputed and undoubtedly effective at preventing childhood abductions. "I have never done a program where someone hasn't come up to me afterwards to tell me what happened to them," she says. "They are now empowered to similarly help prevent children from being victimized. For a long time now we've been inundated with letters from parents telling us that we saved their child's life because they were able to defend against a predator."

While she's confident that her work is helping many families, Sophia continues her quest to reach more families and dispel the common myths. "The most common misconception parents have is they think the predator will be someone they don't know or someone that will be obvious to them. Now with the sex offender registries that many communities have, parents will search for their ZIP code and only pay attention to the individuals that come up on the list, not those that fly under the radar and have yet to be caught. I have to show them that it could be anyone, even someone close to them, just like in my case."

For Sophia, her quest not only gives families valuable information but also a feeling of empowerment and strength with sincerity and compassion. "People say they can't believe I do this for free. Unless you've gone through it, it's hard to explain to someone how passion takes over and gives you a purpose. But I always let them know that just because you've been victimized you don't need to dwell in victim mentality. If you channel your energies to help others rise above atrocities, you become victorious."

TERI WESTERMAN
Co-Founder
Physically Handicapped Actors and Musical Artists League (PHAMALy)

"Some people have dreamed about doing this but never had the chance. We wanted to give them that chance."

When Teri Westerman graduated from high school, she had no idea what she would be up against. All she wanted to be was a performer. Since her younger days she had been singing, and more recently had become interested in acting. Until she graduated from high school, finding roles had not been a problem; she had participated in several performances in both junior high and high school. But when it came time to look beyond her school to Colorado's artistic community, she learned that even getting an audition was almost impossible.

Teri's interest in the arts started at a very young age. As a child she happened to see a performance of *The Nutcracker* on television and from that day on it was a dream of hers to play a part in that ballet. For many years after that, her dream remained that—just a dream. Sure, she enjoyed music and singing, but she was neither an actor nor a dancer. What helped Teri eventually see that her dream of being in a musical was possible was the inspiration of a teacher.

In the eighth grade, it was her choir teacher that showed her the possibilities. "I had an amazing choir teacher," Teri says. "One day she said we were going to do a musical. I kind of laughed when she said that because I knew I could sing, but I didn't know I could act." Once Teri tried her hand at acting, she was hooked. "That's where the love of theater really started. It was an outlet I had never had the chance to explore."

Teri's interest continued through high school. When she graduated, she thought she could finally spend all of her time doing what she loved. She found, though, that it would not be as easy as it had been when she was in high school. "You weren't even given serious consideration because of your disability," she says.

For someone as talented as Teri, it seemed odd that she would not have numerous opportunities to pursue a career in theater. But the sad reality she faced was that, instead of being recognized for her talent, theater companies and casting directors only saw her disability—a disability that confined her to a wheelchair.

It was tough for Teri to face the opposition whenever she tried to audition, knowing that her talent did not seem to matter to those who refused her the chance to perform. But for Teri, the fact that she was in a wheelchair and had been in one her entire life had not stopped her from pursuing her passion before, and she was not going to let it stop her now.

Fortunately for Teri, she was not the only one going through this experience. A group of five friends she went to school with were facing the same challenges. It was one of those friends who had what seemed to be a radical idea.

"After we had all spent some time trying to audition and become a part of some of the local theater companies, one of my friends called me saying she had a great idea," Teri recalls. That idea was to start their own theater company for actors with disabilities. "She said that since no one would look at us seriously, we should start our own company."

Not knowing much about starting a theater company or even running one, Teri and her friends got together to think about their idea and to discuss some of the questions that went along with starting a company with such a unique mission. "We had to think about whether it should include able-bodied people or just people with disabilities, and whether it should include both mental and physical disabilities." Although that meeting did help them clarify what they wanted, it would still be several years before these ideas would become more than just ideas.

The next time Teri received a telephone call from that friend saying it was time to start the theater company, Teri was ready to begin. It all seemed a bit overwhelming with all the work they would have to put into creating such an organization, but the help they needed was there.

With the hope that physically disabled individuals would have an opportunity to pursue their passion of acting, Teri and her group of friends began to create an organization that was long overdue. To reflect the purpose of the new theater company and the strong bond that its members would have, they settled on a name that would illustrate that bond.

"We actually came up with the word 'family' before we came up with the full name of the company," she says, "because we wanted it to be an organization with a supportive environment and very few egos." The year was 1989, and PHAMALy (Physically Handicapped Actors and Musical Artists League) was officially born.

As with any organization, funding was a big part of what this new theater company would need in order to produce shows. When someone suggested they apply for a grant from one of Colorado's arts organizations, Teri was more cautious than optimistic. "We said we would just apply and see what happens," she says. "We thought they would probably send the application back to us and tell us that we were missing something or needed more information. Instead they sent us the money."

That money—a $3,000 grant from Very Special Arts Colorado—meant that PHAMALy could start planning its first production. The next step for PHAMALy was to start work on its first show. Although they had done a lot to get to this point, there were still some unforeseen challenges that Teri and the group would have to work through before they could make their stage debut.

In 1990, the group settled on *Guys and Dolls* as PHAMALy's first production. The show called for a cast of about thirty actors, but they ended up having only fifteen. "We lacked a lot of the things we needed," Teri says, "like more money and more actors, but we worked with what we had. Many of the actors played several parts. To save money we made our own costumes and props."

Even making the costumes proved to be a difficult task. "Costuming for someone in a wheelchair is very difficult. If they can't get out of the wheelchair you have to put the costume around them." Another challenge was finding a place to rehearse and perform. The location they went with was the high school auditorium where many of them got their start in acting. This location was not chosen for sentimental reasons, but because of the stigma that Teri and the group faced as disabled actors.

"Our first performance was in our old high school auditorium because it was the only place that would let us on the stage," she says. "Everywhere else we tried to go denied us because of the perceived liability of putting disabled people on stage."

For such a non-traditional theater company, there were many issues that PHAMALy had to deal with that other theater companies would never have to face. "There are always things to think about," Teri says. "For the hearing impaired actors we had to come up with a way for them to feel the music. For the visually impaired we had to teach them how to dance. One thing over the years that has always been a challenge is teaching a blind person how to make facial expressions."

Another of those issues arose from having a lead actor who was blind. "In our first production, our leading lady was blind, so we had to deal with how to keep her from walking too close to the edge of the stage. For the first few productions we strung a heavy fishing line across the front of the stage so she and the other blind cast members could feel it before walking too close to the edge. In later productions, instead of using the string, we put a textured floor layer at the edge of the stage so the actors could feel that."

With the success of that first production, PHAMALy continued to use the few resources it had to give disabled actors a chance that others had denied them. In its third year of existence, Teri took over as chairman of the board of directors and used the frustration she had before starting PHAMALy to move the organization forward. Part of that effort meant finding a permanent rehearsal and performance space that would be easily accessible for the actors.

Hoping to find the support they needed, Teri met with the director of the Denver Center Theater Company who saw first-hand Teri's passion for PHAMALy. "I met with the director of the theater to see if we could get rehearsal space," Teri says. "I went on and on talking about PHAMALy because I'm so passionate about it. When I finally finished talking, he chuckled and said, 'You had me in the first five minutes—of course we have space for you.'"

The space that he showed to Teri was perfect. "It was a round theater, and it was such a good fit because the floor was the stage and the seating goes up around it, which makes the stage fully accessible." Being able to use this space and being affiliated with a well-known theater company gave PHAMALy the push it needed to continue growing.

Since the first production in 1990, when the cast members had to play two roles because there were not enough actors, the company has grown so much and become so popular that now more actors audition than there are parts. "We've grown so much that we can no longer cast everyone that auditions. Getting a part in one of our productions is truly based on the audition and nothing else."

As one of PHAMALy's biggest fans, Teri is quick to point out that the success of the company is not just due to its unique mission, but also to the talent of the actors. "For people that have never come to one of our shows they come with the idea that it will be a nice little show because it's disabled people," Teri says. "But ten minutes into the show they won't be thinking that anymore because they will see how talented we are."

Outside of her work with PHAMALy, Teri continues to pursue her passion. That passion has led her to become a competitive wheelchair ballroom dancer internationally and led her to be crowned Miss Wheelchair Colorado in 2000. Although you will probably never see her wearing her crown, her childhood dream of being in *The Nutcracker* came true a few years ago when she played the part of the Snow Queen. All of this has been possible because of her belief that there is no limit to what she can do with the love and support of her PHAMALy.

ANNE WHITMAN, PH.D.
Founder and President
Jonathan O. Cole, M.D. Mental Health
Consumer Resource Center

*"My illness has become a tool for teaching and
supporting others with mental illness."*

For the millions of Americans suffering from some form of mental illness, finding treatment and recovering can be a lifelong process. For Anne Whitman, this process of recovery included the creation of a mental health center that now serves as a national model for treating sufferers of mental illnesses.

At the age of 33, Anne Whitman seemed to have it all. With a high-powered job leading a premier program at Harvard University and the responsibility for garnering several million dollars in revenue a year, Anne was a rare force of ingenuity and talent who was undoubtedly destined to make a significant mark in the worlds of business and academia. In addition to her professional success, a newborn daughter and a successful husband propelled Anne to what many would call an ideal life.

Shortly after the birth of her daughter, something unexpected happened. Anne began to experience post-partum depression—a form of depression that affects many mothers for a short period after the birth of a child. For her, the depression lingered and soon led to episodes of psychosis. Thinking that her home and office were under surveillance by the FBI, she went to her employer sharing her concerns and requesting that the police be called. She heeded the dismissive advice given to her—that she should see a psychiatrist—and then took a six-week break from her job to recover. The psychosis was temporarily ameliorated by the break, but she was unaware of the depth of her illness.

Upon returning to work after the leave of absence, Anne was greeted with an ultimatum that if she did not resign she would be terminated. There would be no time for healing or discussions of ways to work through the problems that led to this point, only the tough reality of how people with mental illnesses can all too often be stigmatized and disregarded.

Losing her job would not even be the worst news Anne would hear. Within a short period of time she lost custody of her daughter, went through a divorce, and lost many of her friends. Sitting isolated in her home, Anne found that the life that had once seemed ideal was now anything but.

Loneliness can be a bitter pill for someone suffering from a mental illness, but love and support can provide a light of hope that things will get better. The first step in Anne's long road to recovery was her family. Her parents traveled from several states away to come to her aid and help her get the treatment that would allow her to return to a productive life. For the many families beset with such circumstances, finding treatment for an area of health care that is often kept quiet and highly stigmatized can be a maze of confusion. This was no different in Anne's case.

With nowhere to turn, her illness became a cloud of secrecy that hung over her family. It was only through determination and the belief that this illness would not be the end of her that she was able to find what would finally work for her.

With more than just a need for medication, Anne formed a close bond with the doctors and caregivers who played a role in her recovery. One such bond showed itself in the emergency ward of a hospital. One of the primary doctors working at that hospital was also caring for his wife, who was giving birth at that time in the same hospital. Between his wife's labor contractions, this doctor would leave the delivery room to care for Anne and continue her treatment program. It was these expressions of care that encouraged Anne to regain custody of the daughter she had lost due to the onset of her mental illness.

"Medications brought me back to reality," she says, "but it was a committed group of family, friends, therapists, and peers who brought me back to life."

While finding effective treatment was more than enough of a challenge for Anne, getting herself back on her feet and regaining the trust of her daughter was another. Balancing time between raising her daughter and completing her treatment program proved difficult.

A few months after beginning her treatment program, Anne felt ready to step back into the workforce. In an employment counseling session for people with psychiatric disabilities at the Boston University Center for Psychiatric Rehabilitation, Anne was asked to complete an exercise that included searching through job announcements in a local newspaper and circling those that were most appealing to her. The conclusion was telling. Every job that she circled involved starting or creating something new. It became clear that being an entrepreneur and innovator attracted her the most.

Still struggling with her responsibilities as a mother and as a recovering psychiatric patient, Anne tried to enroll her daughter in several childcare facilities in the New England area. Nothing was available. But the determination that had already brought her so far would not let her give up. After putting her daughter on the waiting list at twelve centers, Anne realized that she did not have to wait anymore. She would use her knowledge and talents to create an even better method of childcare for other families that were in her situation.

No more than eight months after being fired from Harvard, Anne was the co-founder of Bright Horizons Children's Centers. Her daughter, who had previously been on the waiting list at other centers, was the first to enroll. Today, there are more than five hundred of these centers providing work-site childcare, and the company is publicly traded on the NASDAQ. There are even several centers that specifically provide childcare for children of the homeless and parents with psychiatric illnesses.

After leaving the childcare company, Anne wondered what she could do to help other sufferers of mental illnesses. She had witnessed how difficult it was to find resources, to get treatment, and to overcome the negative stigma associated with mental illness. She knew there had to be a better way. That better way came when she and Evie Barkin co-founded the Jonathan O. Cole, M.D. Mental Health Consumer Resource Center located at McLean Hospital.

Born out of Anne's own frustrations and difficulty finding treatment and overcoming the negative stigma, the Cole Center would be a place of support for people with mental illnesses. It would be unusual in that there, patients would receive guidance from medical professionals as well as from individuals who had suffered from and overcome mental illnesses.

Even with Anne's dedication to the idea of starting this type of resource center, there was still the negative stigma associated with psychiatric illnesses that would have to be overcome to make this center a reality.

Upon approaching a local hospital to find a location, she was rebuffed. But nothing could stop Anne—mental illness had not, and one setback in her plan to create a resource center would not either. Within two weeks she had the space at McLean Hospital—one chair and a lamp. Next they were given an office in the basement and then later moved to a space in the cafeteria.

In describing the experience of starting the Cole Center with limited space, Anne says, "We started small and moved up as we gained acceptance."

Not only does the Cole Center serve as a place to seek support and to learn more about mental illnesses, but it is also completely staffed by people who have dealt successfully with their own mental illnesses. From the president of the center to the volunteers, the staff is able to provide a very direct and hands-on approach while serving as examples of hope for those currently seeking treatment.

Walking into the Cole Center on any given day, you may find a family reading information or talking with a counselor about how best to care for a loved one. You may find a group in the cafeteria getting together to break their isolation and connect with one another through their own mental illnesses to forge new, healthy friendships. The small group of teenagers you may see meeting with their peer educators are discussing their progress in school and how to build and maintain positive relationships. In another corner of the cafeteria you may see several individuals writing about their own personal struggles with mental health in hopes of breaking the stigma and giving hope to current sufferers. The soft sound of music you hear that you think may be coming from a radio is actually a group of musicians coming together for an afternoon of expression through song.

And finally, you notice a woman standing at the center of it all taking a deep breath and showing quiet satisfaction, the kind that only someone who has been through darkness and seen light can have. Now the light Anne Whitman found touches every corner of the Cole Center and the many families and individuals it serves.

INDEX OF ORGANIZATIONS

Charmaney Bayton
Hope's Nest
www.hopesnest.org
P.O. Box 8520
Calabasas, California 91372

Shirlene Cooper
New York City AIDS Housing Network
www.nycahn.org
80-A Fourth Avenue
Brooklyn, New York 11217
(877) 615-2217

Shelly Cyprus
Service of the Emergency Aid Resource Center for the
Homeless (SEARCH)
www.searchproject.org
2505 Fannin
Houston, Texas 77002
(713) 739-7752

Matt D'Arrigo
A Reason To Survive (ARTS)
www.artsurvive.org
2820 Roosevelt Road, Suite 106
San Diego, California 92106
(619) 297-ARTS (2787)

Fay DeAvignon
Angels of Hope
www.angelsofhopeuganda.org
(508) 653-0764

Bob LoBue
Visions Recovery
www.visionsrecoveryplay.org

Sylvia Godfrey
Florida Keys Juvenile Services
www.islandhome.org

Elissa Montanti
The Global Medical Relief Fund
www.globemed.org
239 Fingerboard Road
Staten Island, New York 10305
(866) 734-GMRF (4673)

Jose Morales
Jovenes 24
www.jovenes24.org
(718) 458-0108

Tom Prichard
Sudan Sunrise
www.sudansunrise.org
8643 Hauser Court, Suite 240
Lenexa, Kansas 66215
(913) 599-0800

Emma Rhodes, Ed.D.
Emma Rhodes Education & Multipurpose Center
1815 Wright Avenue
Little Rock, Arkansas
(501) 374-5712

Johana Scot
Parent Guidance Center
www.parentguidancecenter.org
1300 S. Frazier, Suite 215
Conroe, Texas 77301
(800) 542-0615

Robina Suwol
California Safe Schools
www.calisafe.org
P.O. Box 2756
Toluca Lake, California 91610
(818) 785-5515

Sophia Key West
Mothers Against Predators
www.goodknight.org/MAP/home.html
P.O. Box 901
Beltsville, Maryland 20704
(301) 595-8989

Teri Westerman
Physically Handicapped Actors & Musical Artists League
(PHAMALY)
www.phamaly.org
P.O. Box 44216
Denver, Colorado 80201
(303) 575-0005

Anne Whitman, Ph.D.
Jonathan O. Cole, M.D. Mental Health Consumer
Resource Center
www.coleresourcecenter.org
McLean Hospital
115 Mill Street
Belmont, Massachusetts 02478
(617) 855-3298

RESOURCES TO HELP YOU BE THE DIFFERENCE

Charity Focus
www.charityfocus.org

Do Something
www.dosomething.org

Everyday Giving Blog
www.everydaygivingblog.org

Kiva
www.kiva.org

Razoo
www.razoo.com

Network For Good
www.networkforgood.org/volunteer

Volunteer Match
www.volunteermatch.org

Do you know someone who is being the difference in your community? The author would appreciate hearing from you: dgraham@booksallaround.org.

Made in the USA